Much ado about
SHAKESPEARE

The life and times of William Shakespeare – a literary picture book

DONOVAN BIXLEY

upstart press

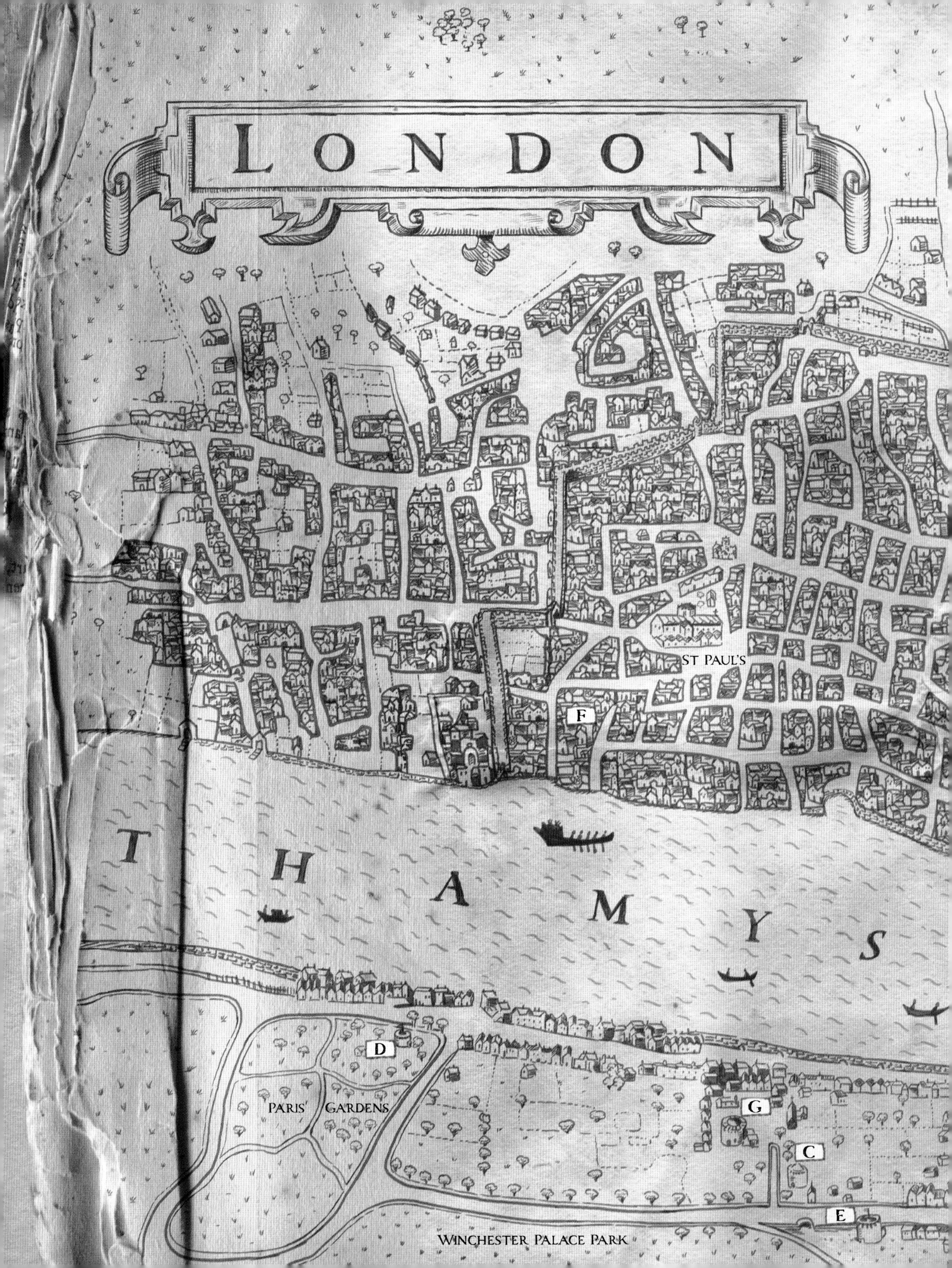

LONDON
ST PAUL'S
F
T H A M Y S
D
PARIS' GARDENS
G
C
E
WINCHESTER PALACE PARK

SHOREDITCH

A

B

SPITALFIELD

OORFIELDS

100   200   300

	A.	THE THEATRE
		OPENED 1576
	B.	THE CURTAIN
		OPENED 1577
	C.	THE ROSE
		OPENED 1587
	D.	THE SWAN
		OPENED 1596
	E.	THE GLOBE
		OPENED 1599
	F.	BLACKFRIAR'S THEATRE
		PERFORMANCES BEGAN 1609
	G.	BEAR BAITING RING

THE TOWER

LONDON BRIDGE

SOUTHWARKE

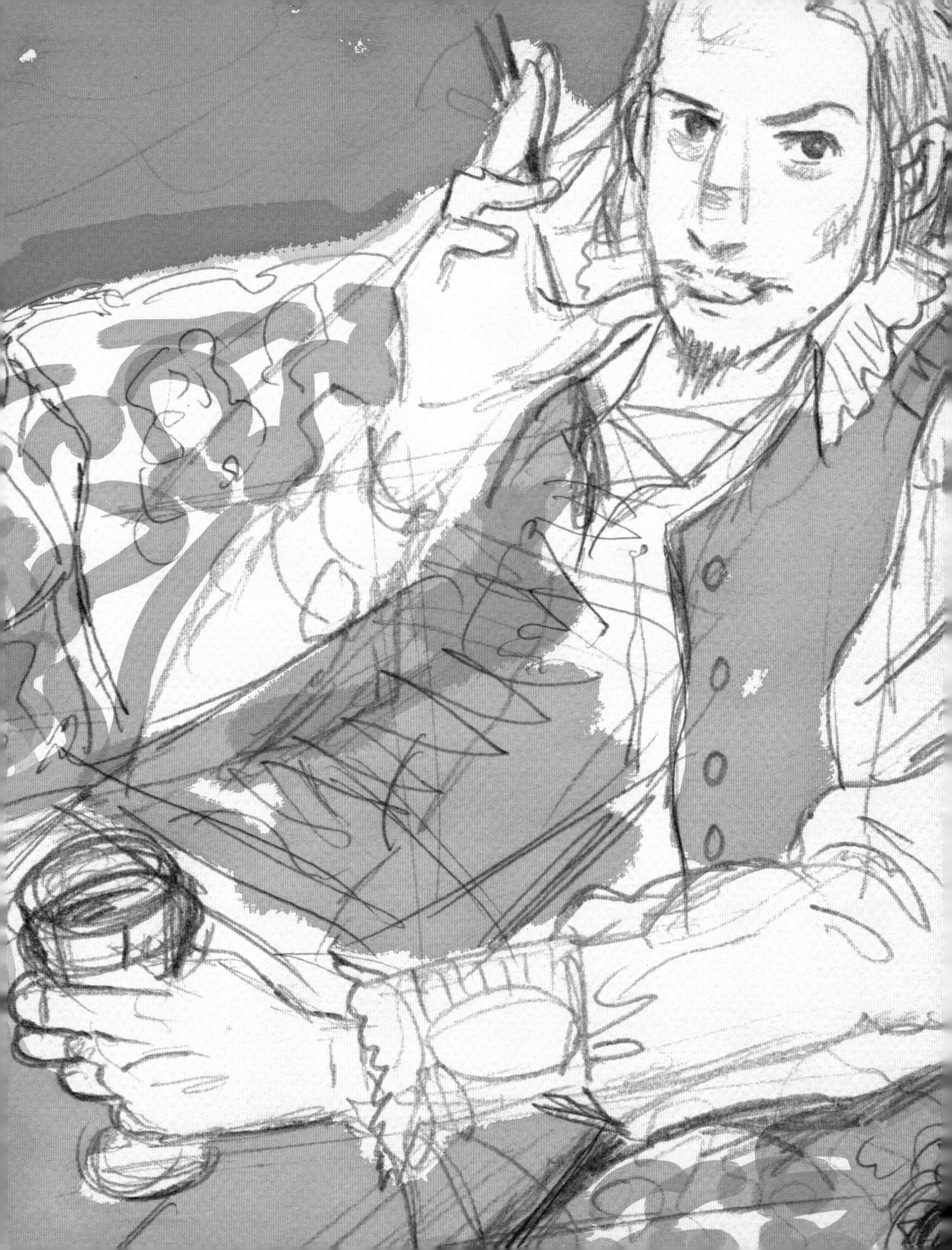

William Shakespeare

has never been sent to the naughty corner of history, or locked in a mouldy cupboard to be rediscovered by future generations. There's never been a period when he was out of fashion. In his lifetime he was incredibly successful, and soon after his death his works were published to the world. As the years passed, he became more famous, and even more famous and still more famous. He is now one of history's truly greatest greats.

It's not because generation upon generation of school children had Shakespeare forced down their throats (or out of their throats, as the case may be), Shakespeare remains not only famous but relevant because every day, across the globe, when grasping for the exact sentiment they need, people find it already there, in phrases that Shakespeare invented. There's 'without rhyme or reason', 'into thin air', 'tongue-tied', 'budge an inch' . . . if this book were a thousand-page tome I could go on and on — but it's not!

Invention and reinvention are the hallmarks of Shakespeare's legacy. From Orson Welles' Nazi *Julius Caesar* to *The Maori Merchant of Venice* to Akira Kurosawa's *Ran* (King Lear) to Disney's

The Lion King (Hamlet), and the thousands of stage interpretations in between, this constant rediscovering and reinterpreting is what keeps Shakespeare alive. With every new telling, a new generation finds new meaning in his words.

Within the traffic of these pages you'll find a new interpretation of Shakespeare's world: a play on words and pictures that attempts, in its small way, to draw back the curtain and shed light on the bright and exuberant world of Shakespeare's life and times. Shakespeare may have had a high, domed forehead, but he was never high-brow; never the snooty artist, locked away from the world — Shakespeare was in the thick of it. A connoisseur of the human condition, he knew how to express every characteristic from the common man to England's queen, and each emotion in between: love, hate, loyalty, betrayal, fear and triumph, beauty, horror, joy and sadness, clarity and madness. He had an intimate understanding that is so universal it will go on speaking across time and culture.

So enjoy the highs and lows, the tongue-in-cheek, the truth and imagination, the life and times of William Shakespeare, in his own words.

There is a history in all men's lives.

HENRY IV PART TWO

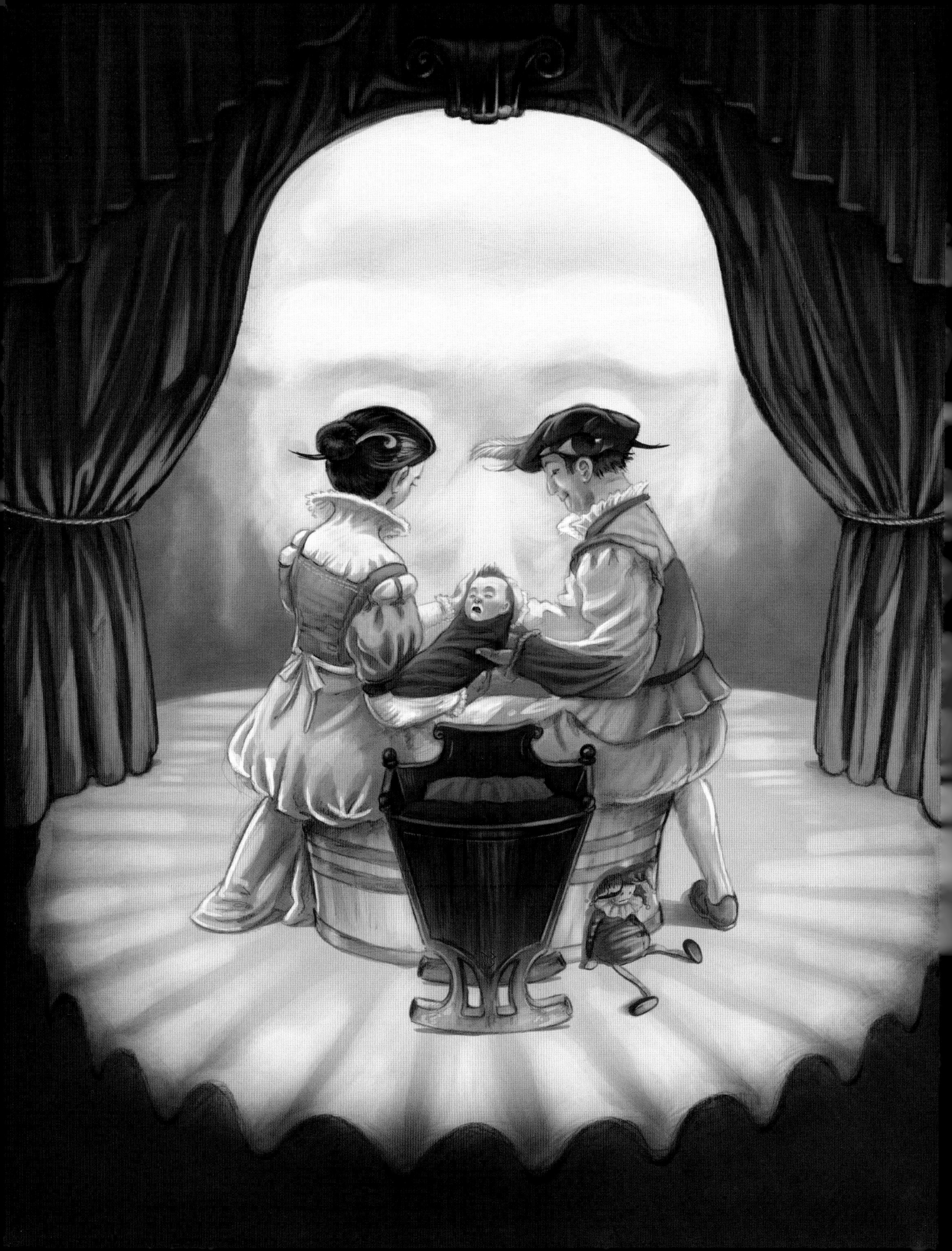

When we are born, we cry that we are come to this great stage of fools.

KING LEAR

Tradition has it that William was born on the 23rd of April 1564. He was the third, but oldest surviving, child of John and Mary Shakespeare. Will's father was one of twenty-three glove makers in the small town of Stratford-upon-Avon. An ambitious young man, John Shakespeare had his sights set on public office and was also a shrewd investor and businessman. Through the Arden family, on his mother's side, Will had a tenuous link to nobility. His father's drive for commercial success and pretensions of gentility were traits Will would take on as he grew.

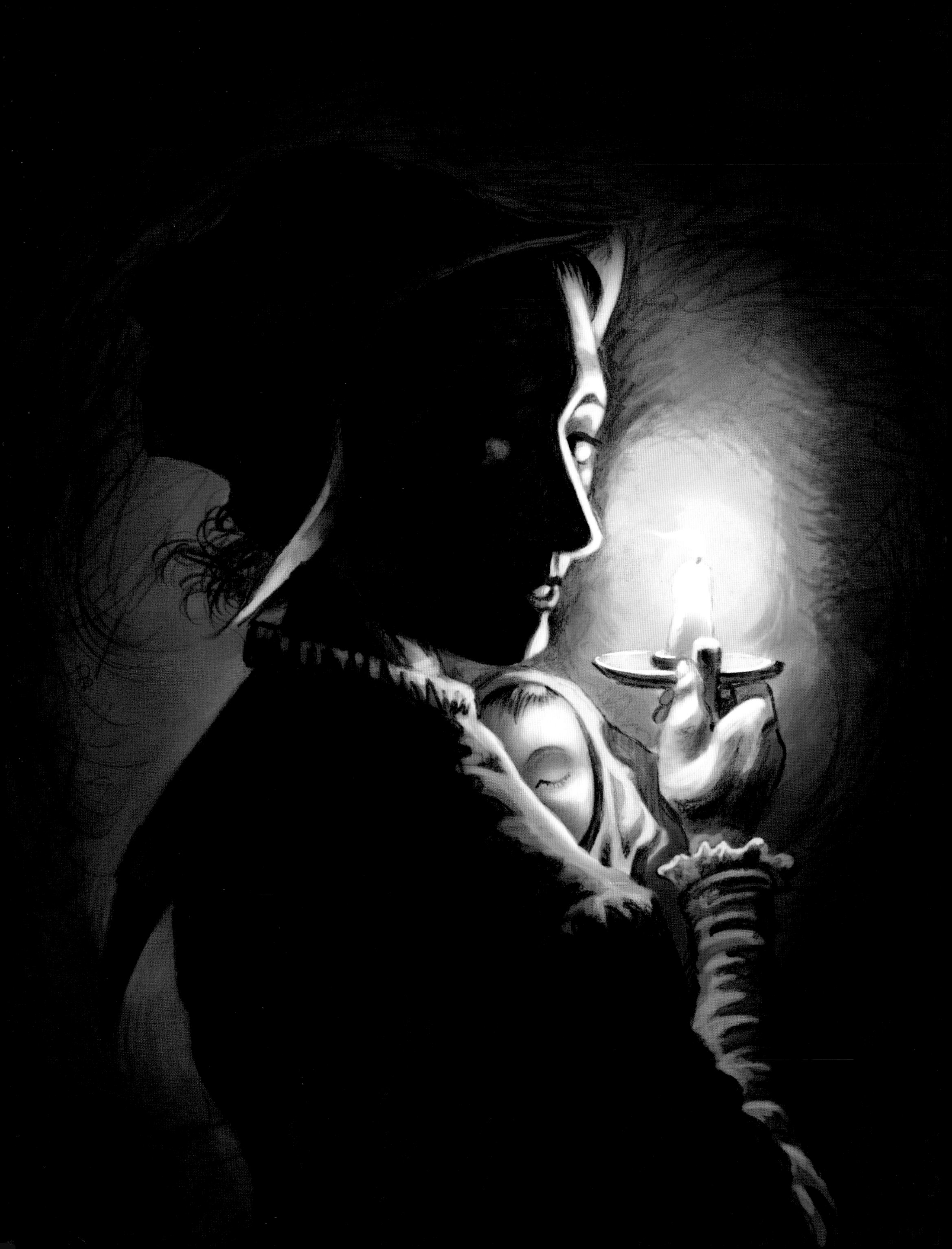

Out, out, brief candle!

MACBETH

One thing's for sure, you had to be pretty tough to make it to your first birthday in Shakespeare's time. In the year of Will's birth, the plague struck Stratford-upon-Avon killing one sixth of the townsfolk.

Although Stratford had an average life expectancy of forty-seven (almost double that of London), child mortality was still huge, with twenty per cent not making it to the end of their first month. Even being born into a prosperous family was no guarantee of survival and Will's poor mother had to bury four of her eight children.

At first the infant, mewling and puking in the nurse's arms.

AS YOU LIKE IT

W̲ill's was a well-to-do family and it would have been common for the baby to have a wet nurse. The usual childhood teething problems were remedied by giving the baby a smooth piece of coral to chew on. Mewling and puking would have been accompanied by more than the usual irritations as even newborns were fitted with that indispensable Elizabethan fashion accessory: the highly starched neck ruff.

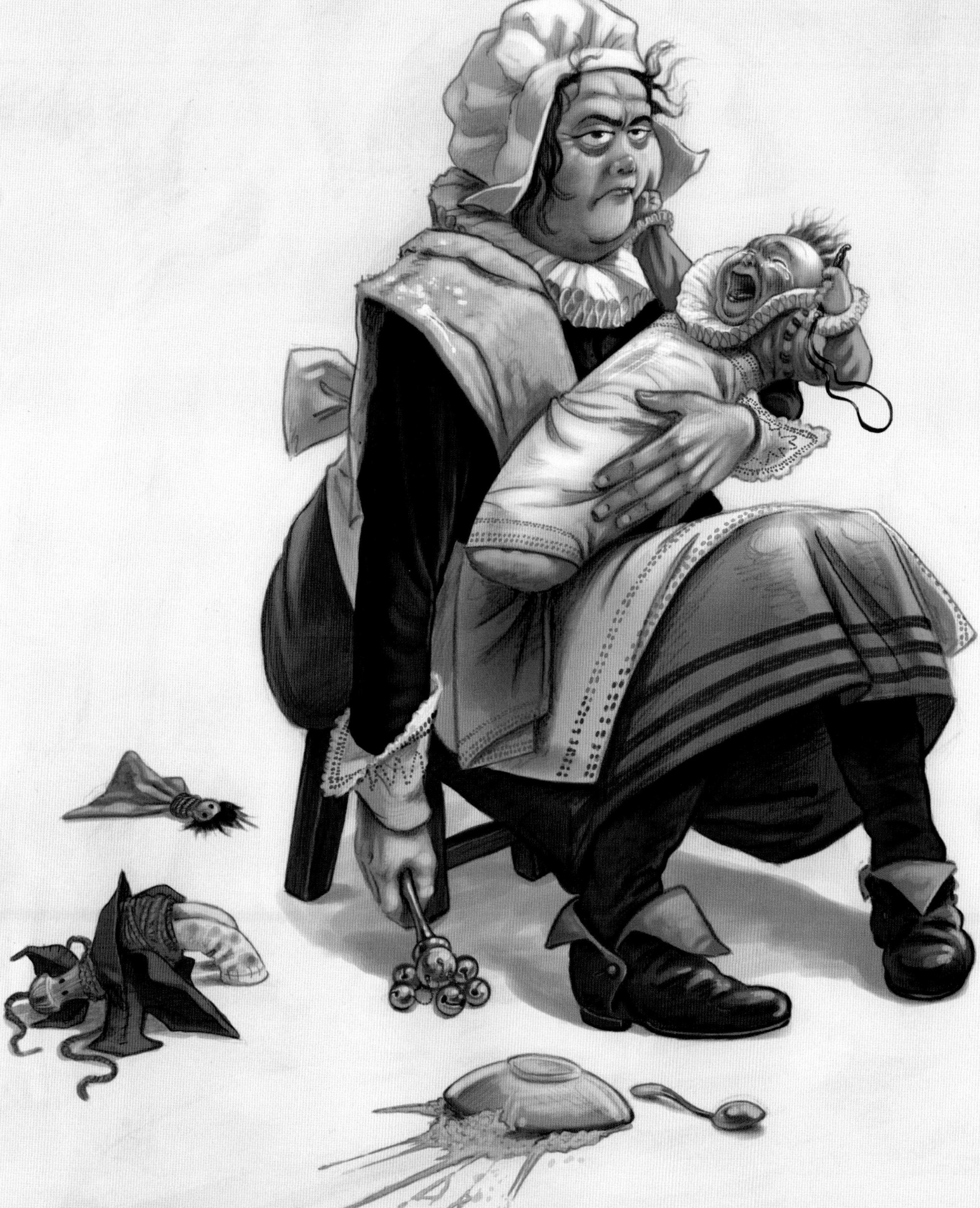

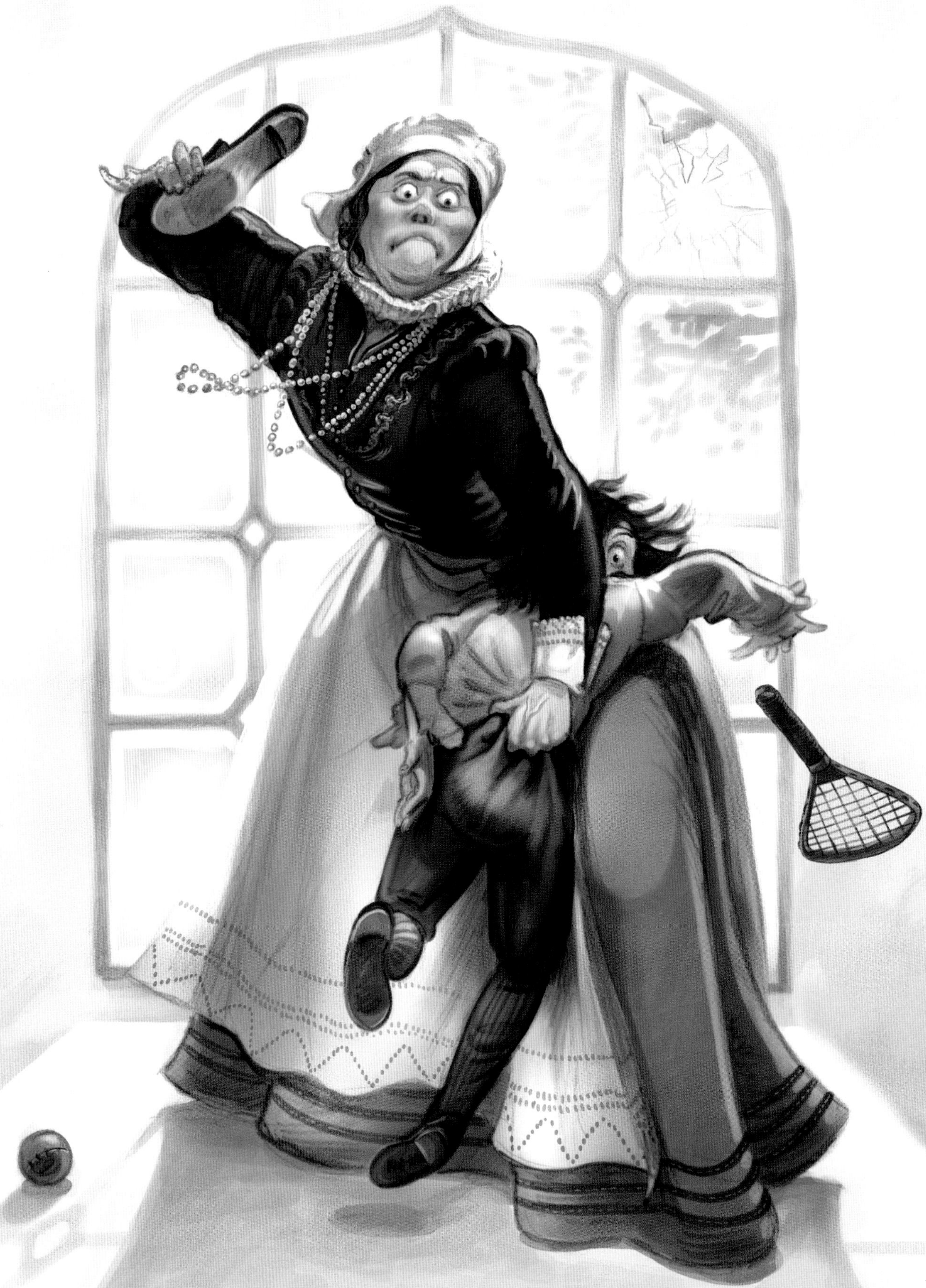

I must be cruel, only to be kind.

HAMLET

Childhood in Elizabethan England was one of strict discipline. Young Will would have risen bright and early to complete his chores before waiting on his parents at breakfast. Parenting, much like the rule of the kingdom, was done with absolute authority. Any uprising or disturbance was met with swift and harsh punishment.

To be, or not to be: that is the question.

HAMLET

Will's father John rose quickly through the ranks of public office, eventually becoming mayor of Stratford-upon-Avon in 1568, when Will was four. As son of a town alderman, Will was entitled to a free education. School was hard work: twelve hours a day, six days a week. Here he was introduced to Latin and became immersed in the plots, language and characters of the Greek and Roman classics. School also involved studies in oratory, composition and performance — the perfect training ground for a budding actor and playwright.

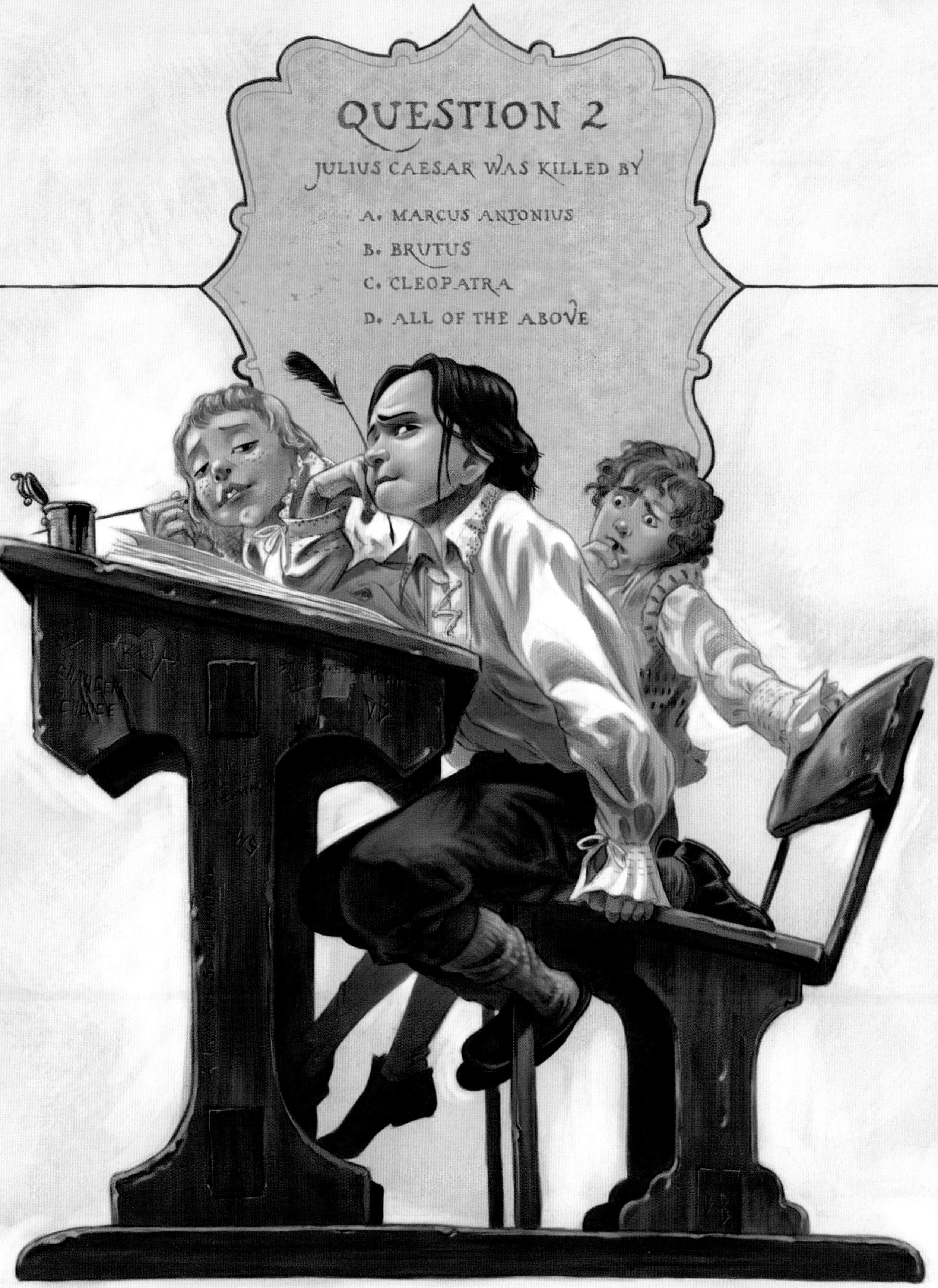
QUESTION 2
JULIUS CAESAR WAS KILLED BY
A. MARCUS ANTONIUS
B. BRUTUS
C. CLEOPATRA
D. ALL OF THE ABOVE

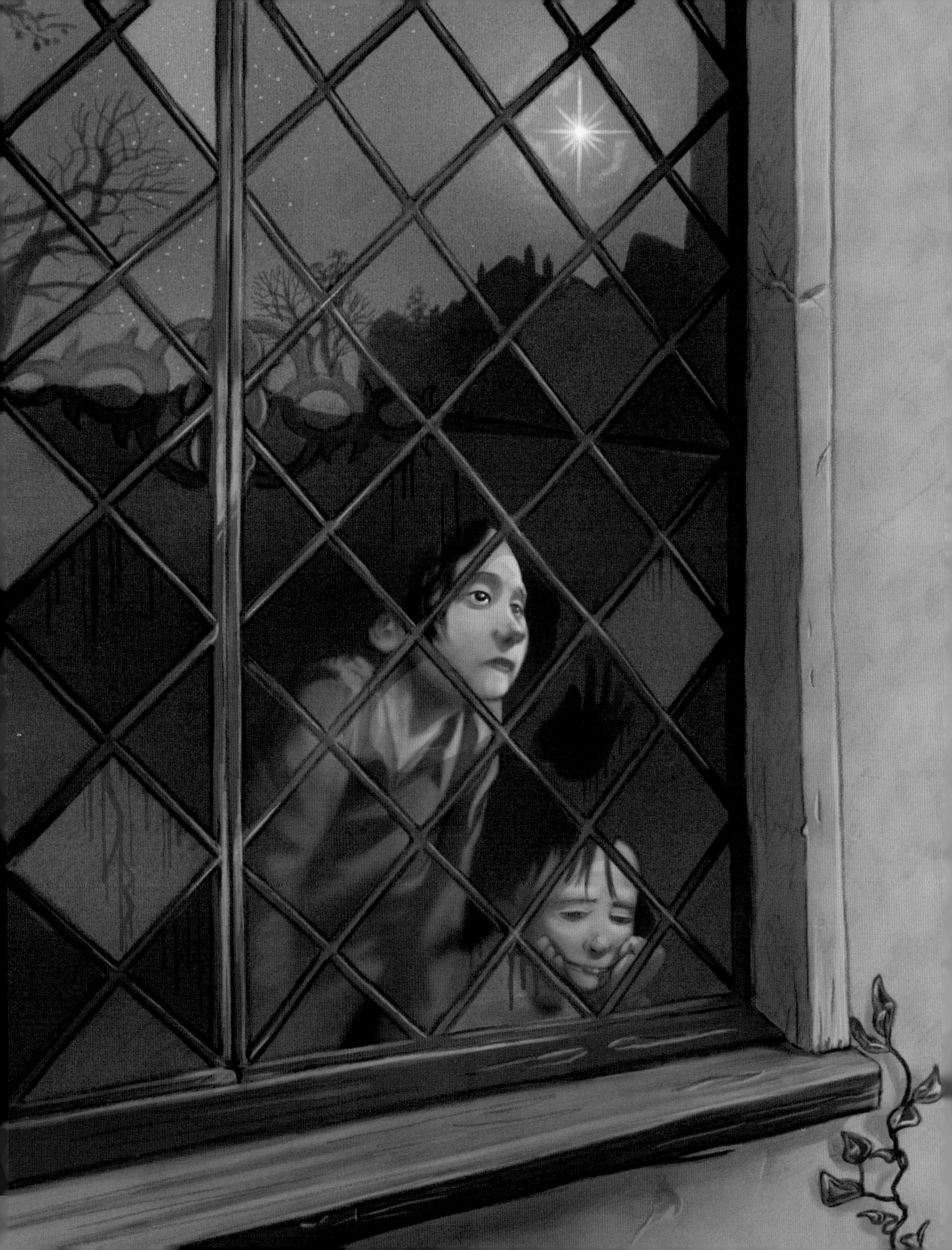

My stars shine darkly over me.

TWELFTH NIGHT

In November 1572 an incredibly portentous event occurred. A supernova appeared in the northern skies, one of only a handful ever seen by the naked eye, and was visible for sixteen months. Will was eight years old, and if he did not witness it first hand, he surely would have experienced the great uneasiness that it caused amongst the townspeople.

The supernova was studied by Danish astronomer Tycho Brahe, and twenty-eight years later Will referenced this supernova in the opening act of his Danish play, *Hamlet*. There are several other connections including the fact that Tycho's observatory was not far from the play's setting, Elsinore Castle.

Audiences of the time would have recognised the ominous sign of a star appearing where no star had been before. It would have set the tone for the tragedy about to unfold on stage. Modern audiences, however, might see another meaning in a bright new 'star' appearing from nowhere.

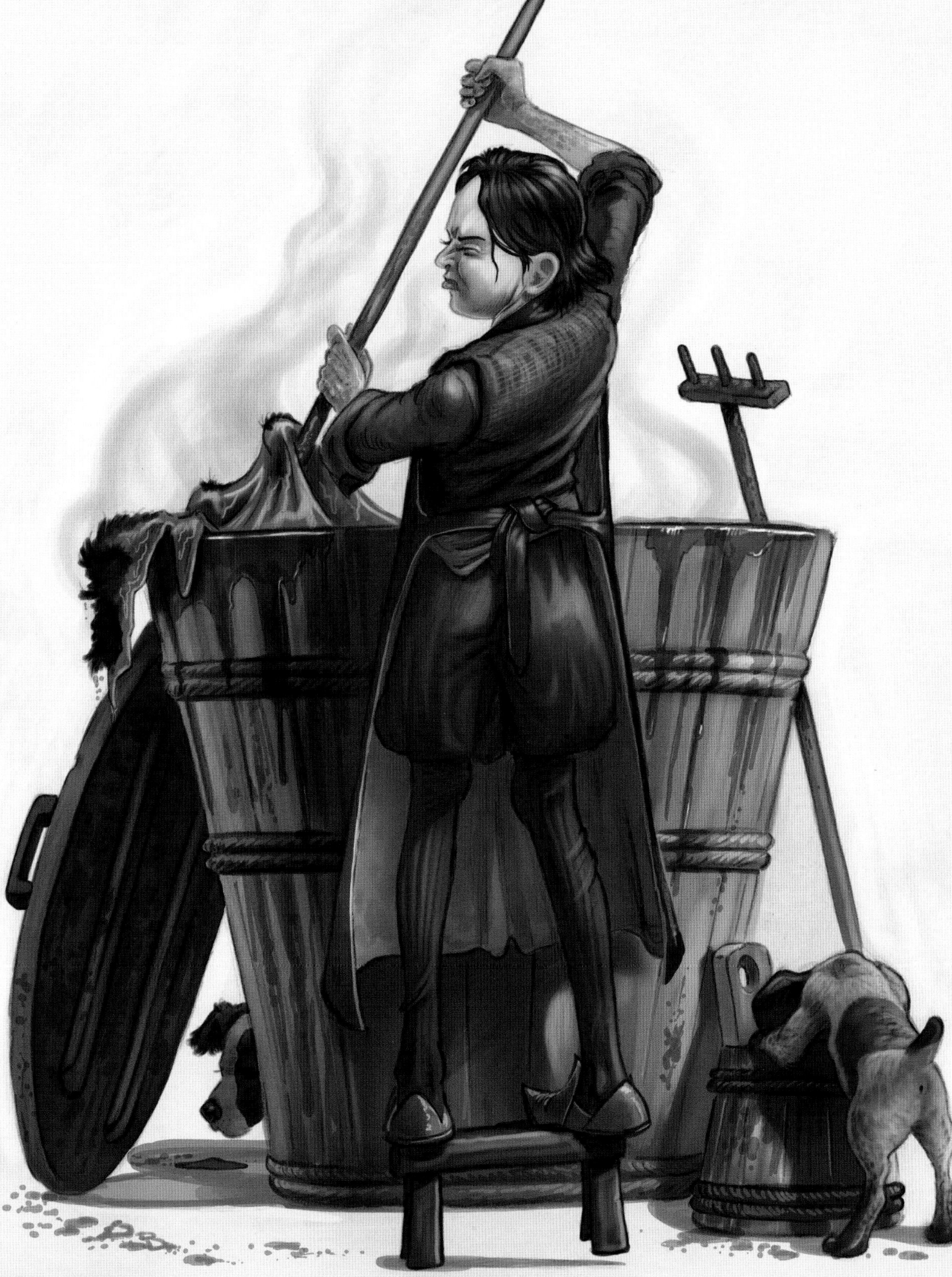

The rankest compound of villainous smell that ever offended nostril.

THE MERRY WIVES OF WINDSOR

Let's face it, life in the sixteenth century was pretty smelly. More so, however, for the Shakespeare family. Dad's trade as a glove maker included tanning and processing all manner of animal skins. This involved soaking the skins in vats of urine then pressing excrement into them, usually dog turds. Everyone was expected to help out with the family business and young Will would have been familiar with all the daily chores which included picking up dog turds and collecting chamber pots around town as well as stirring the vats.

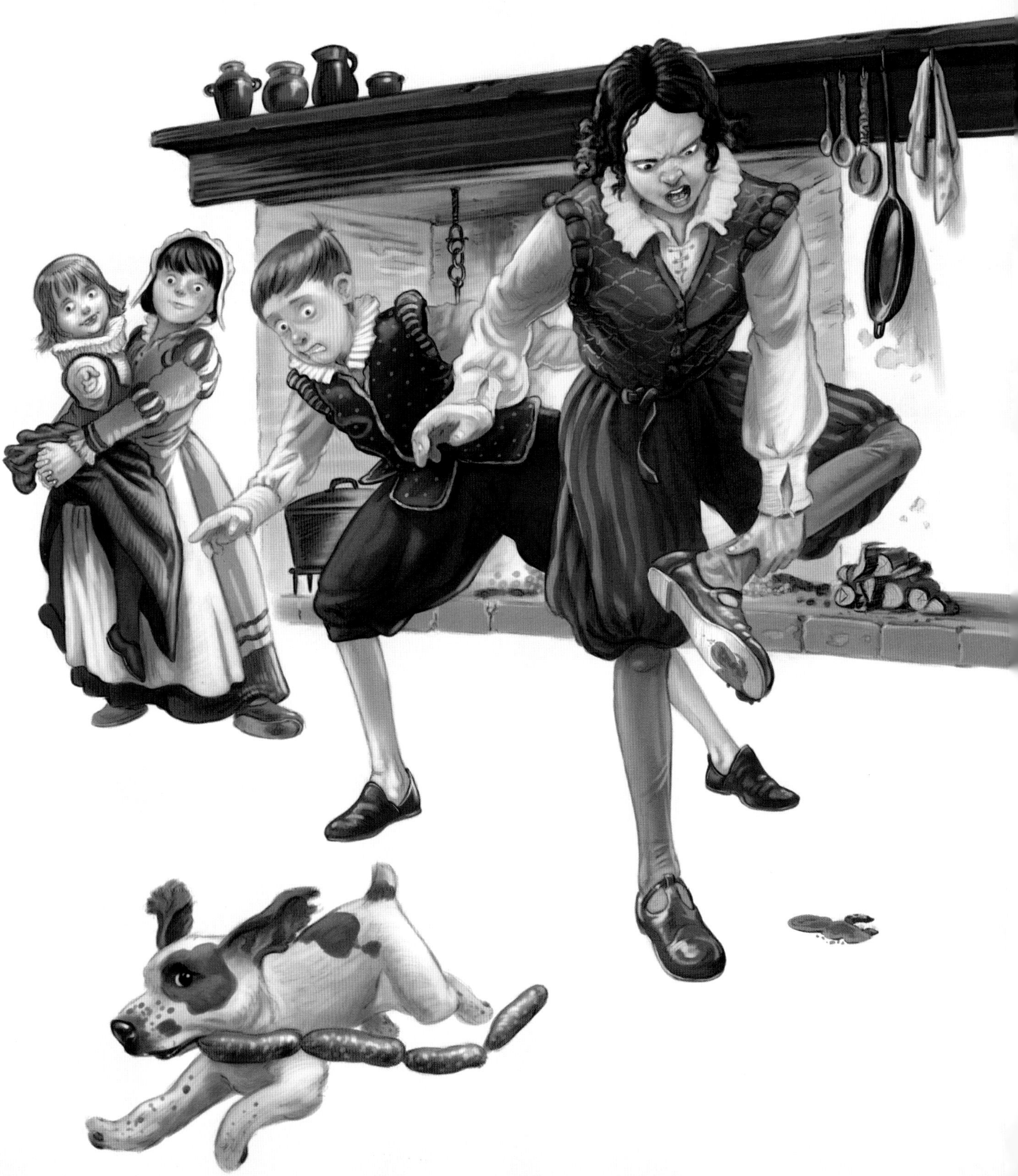

Out, damned spot!
Out, I say!

MACBETH

'Thieving', 'vomit eating', 'poison-toothed', 'whore-son', 'fell curs' — dogs in Shakespeare's plays are anything but the loyal man's-best-friends we think of today. He uses their likeness for his most repulsive characters, including hunchbacked Richard the Third, King Lear's traitorous daughters Regan and Goneril, and that green-eyed racist Iago. Although Shakespeare will sometimes praise the working hound, he is only too quick to slam its grovelling lick and 'candied tongue', sure to remind us that they will just as soon turn on their masters. Perhaps his daily life dealing with dog turds at the tannery had some part to play.

O happy dagger!

ROMEO AND JULIET

It was common for boys to be given a dagger. It was a useful tool carried on their right hip. As they became young men they also wore a rapier or broadsword — and it wasn't just for show. In the streets of the big cities, this armed population of youths often led to violent brawls and riots. It was a brutal time when people lived fast and passionate lives — something Will tapped into with his plays.

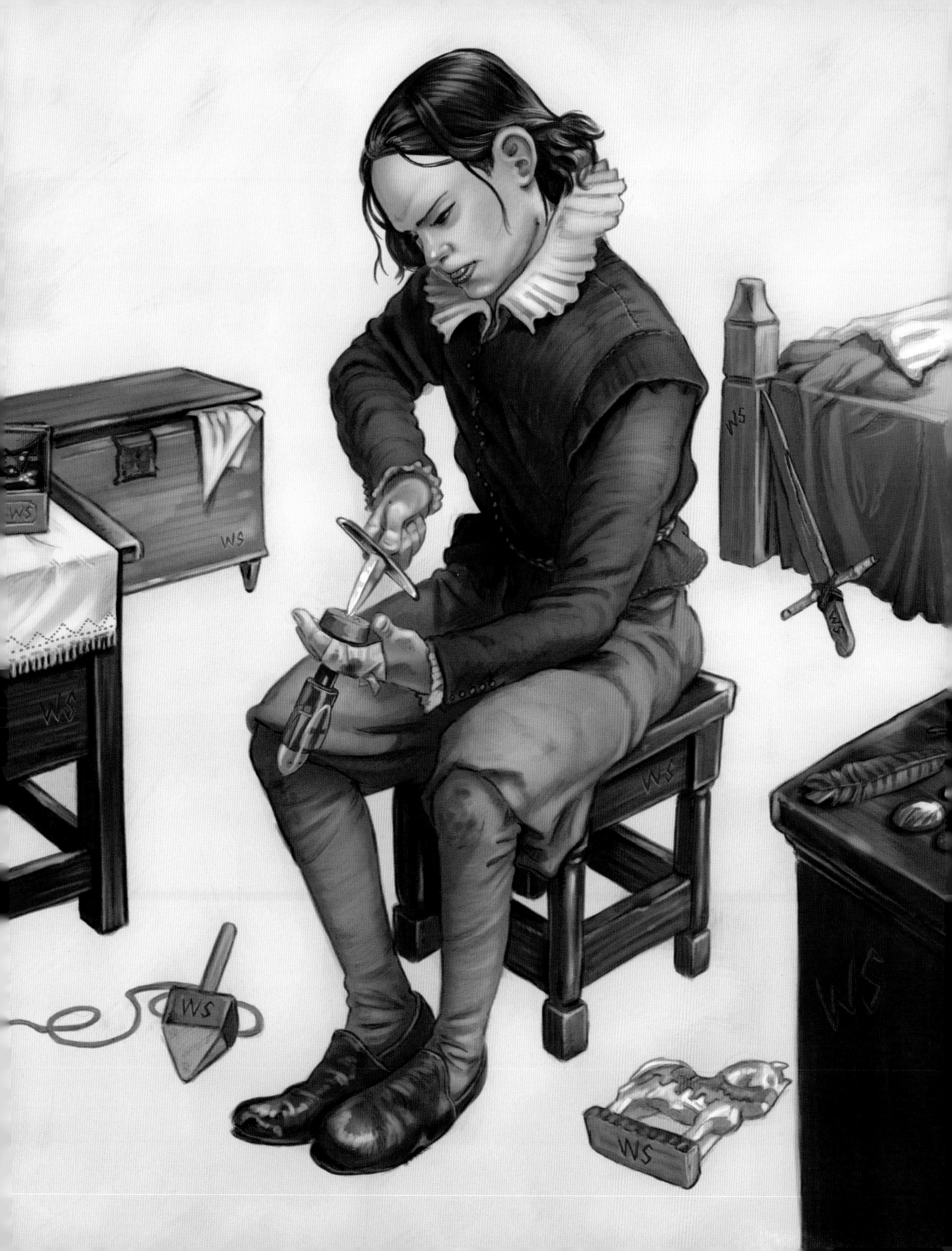
WS

Cry 'Havoc', and let slip the dogs of war.

JULIUS CAESAR

Shakespeare's first biographer, Nicholas Rowe (writing a mere 100 years after Will's death), claimed that the youthful William fell in with bad company who, amongst other unnamed vices, took to repeatedly poaching game from the park lands of one Sir Thomas Lucy, the local lord. Apparently Sir Lucy was so exasperated that he declared war on the coney-catching rascals, prosecuting them to the full extent of the law.

Shakespeare seems to know a fair bit about chasing deer. In his plays he mentions the different types of hounds used and that a crossbow is too noisy and startles the herd.

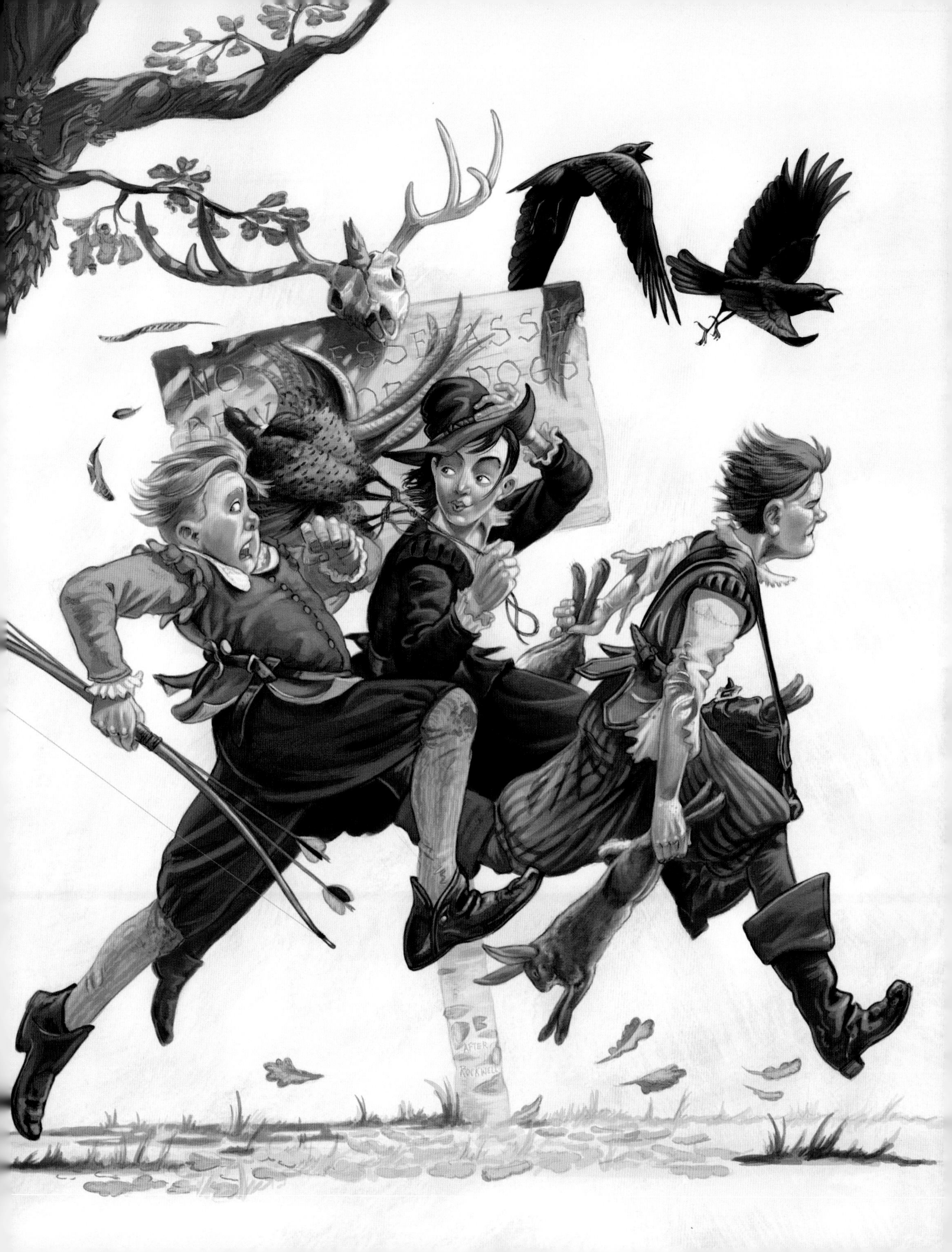
AFTER
ROCKWELL

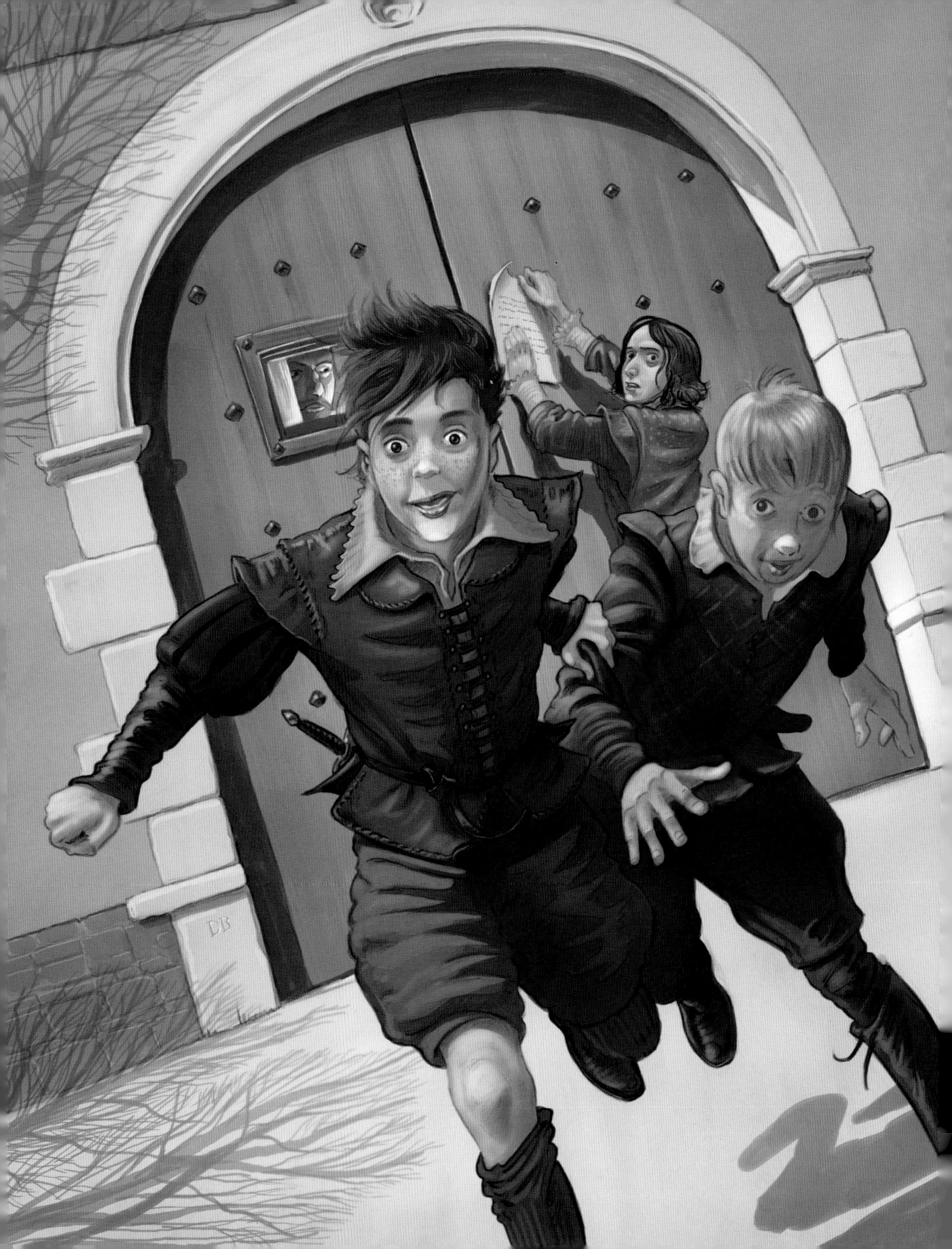

Here are a few of the unpleasant'st words that ever blotted paper!

THE MERCHANT OF VENICE

According to his first biographer, Will was severely punished for poaching Sir Lucy's game, so he decided to retaliate by pinning a vicious ballad to Lucy's gate. It was reputed to have been so strongly and expertly worded that the lord redoubled his persecution, supposedly having Will whipped, imprisoned and eventually driven from Stratford. Whatever the truth behind this anecdote, it is a fact that Sir Lucy was a hard-line Protestant who assisted in rooting out Catholics in Warwickshire, including a particularly harsh persecution of Will's mother's family, the Ardens.

I will make it felony
to drink small beer.

HENRY VI PART TWO

Shakespearean legend claims that Will was renowned, not only as a great poet, but also as a great drinker. One story places Will in the nearby town of Bidford, where our aspiring teenage poet drank so much that he passed out under a local crab-apple tree. By the eighteenth century this hallowed tree had become a tourist shrine known as 'Shakespeare's Crab'.

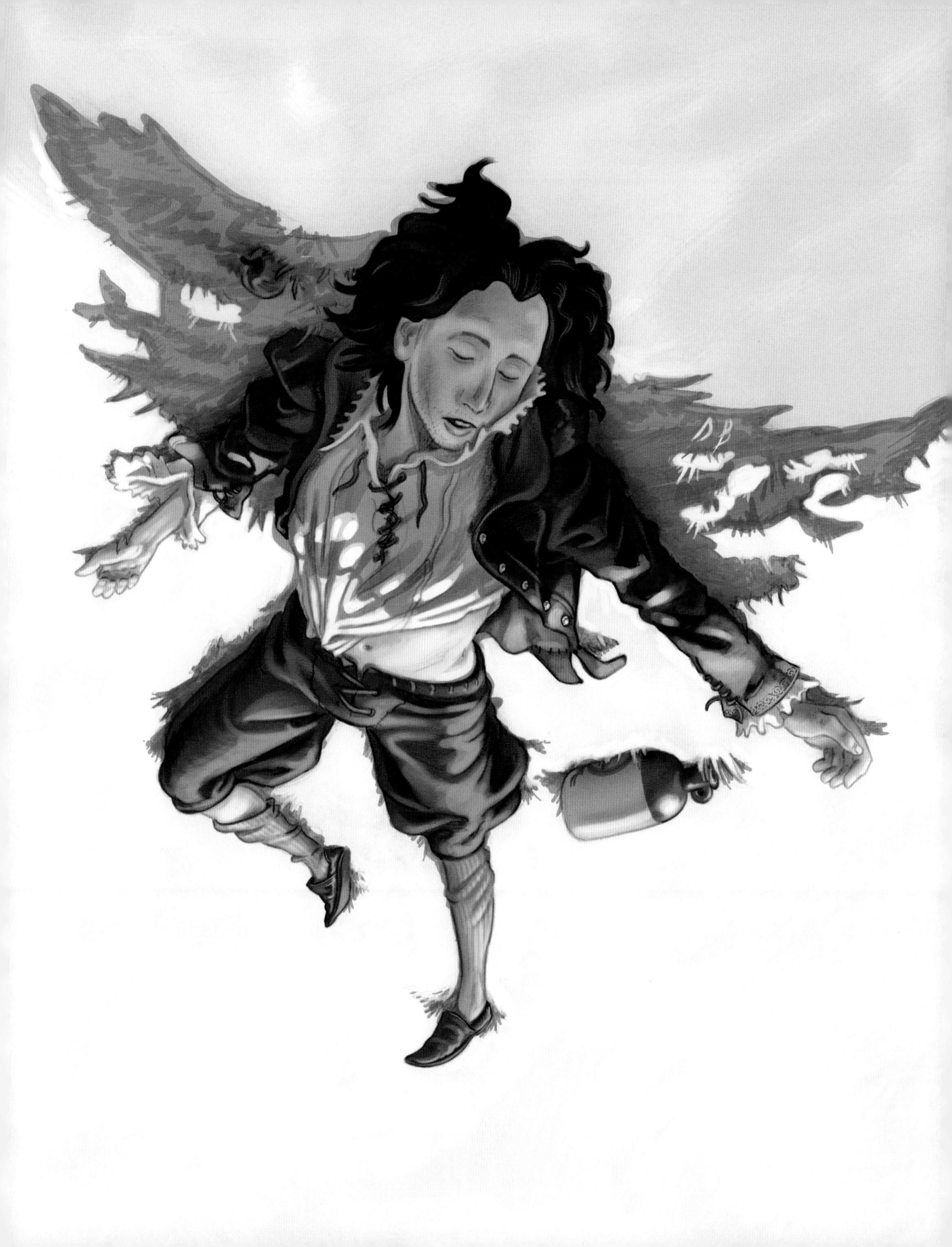

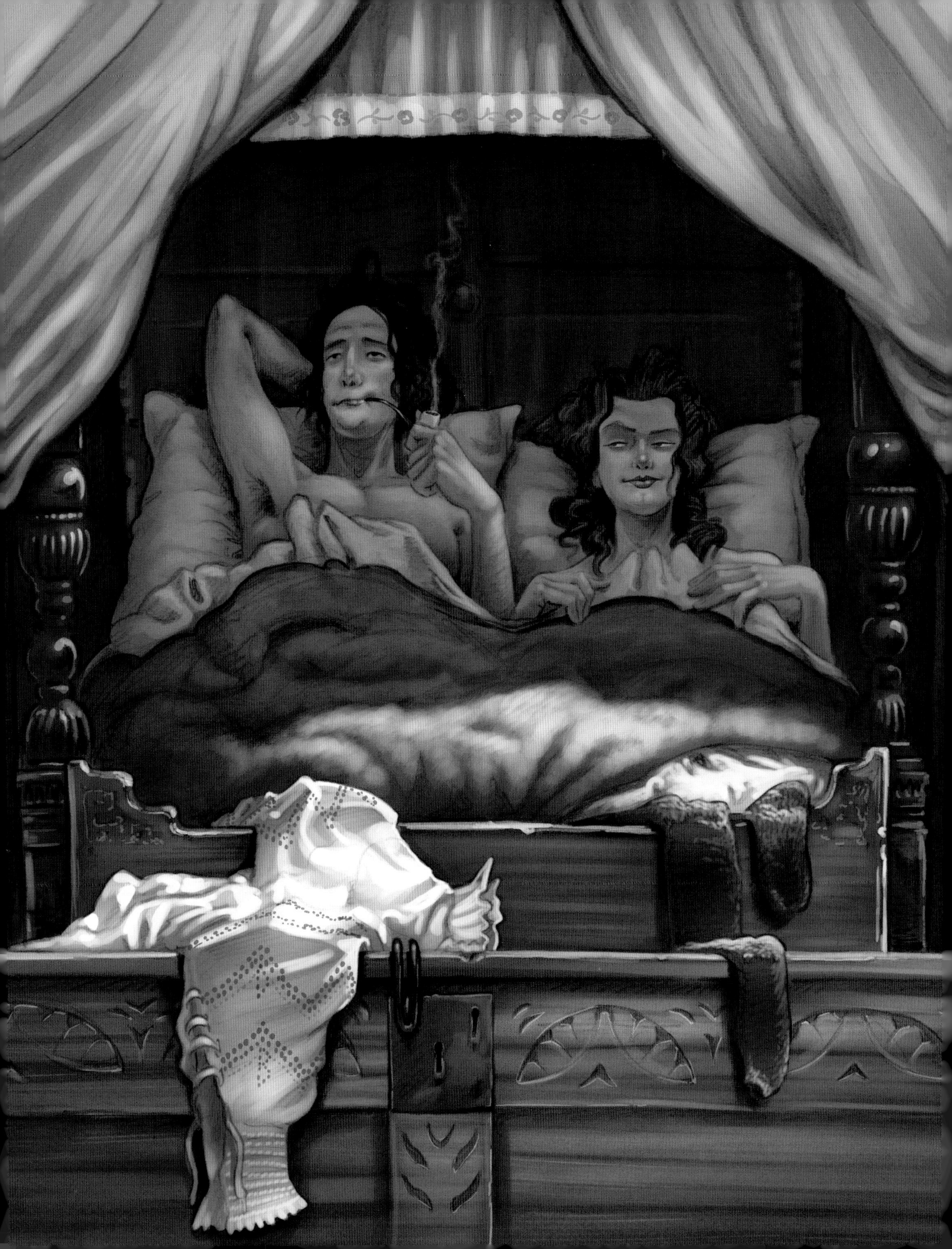

How use doth breed
a habit in a man!

TWO GENTLEMEN OF VERONA

Who knows what Will got up to after he left school? There is so little information regarding many periods of his life. The son of a fellow actor later claimed that Will was a country teacher in his youth. However, we do know what he was getting up to in the summer of 1582: he was practising his future marital duties with his new girlfriend Anne Hathaway. In what is commonly regarded as his first poem, Will writes of a lover who 'sav'd my life'. Anne was eight years older than Will, but what future prospects could she expect from her young Romeo? He obviously had no interest in following his father's trade, and as a young man of letters and learning it is possible that he worked for a time as a law clerk.

Hasty marriage
seldom proveth well.

HENRY VI PART THREE

Will and Anne were married at the end of November 1582. Not surprisingly, the bride was three months' pregnant. This was standard procedure in Elizabethan times. The couple would 'plight their troth' which allowed them to get down to business as long as the wedding came before the child.

They moved into Will's family home on Henley Street. Between Will's parents and his four surviving siblings it was a crowded house with virtually no privacy for the newlyweds. There has been endless debate as to why Will married so young and then chose to spend the majority of his life away from his wife and family, who remained in Stratford. Whatever the case, this hasty marriage was not enough to keep him in Stratford for long.

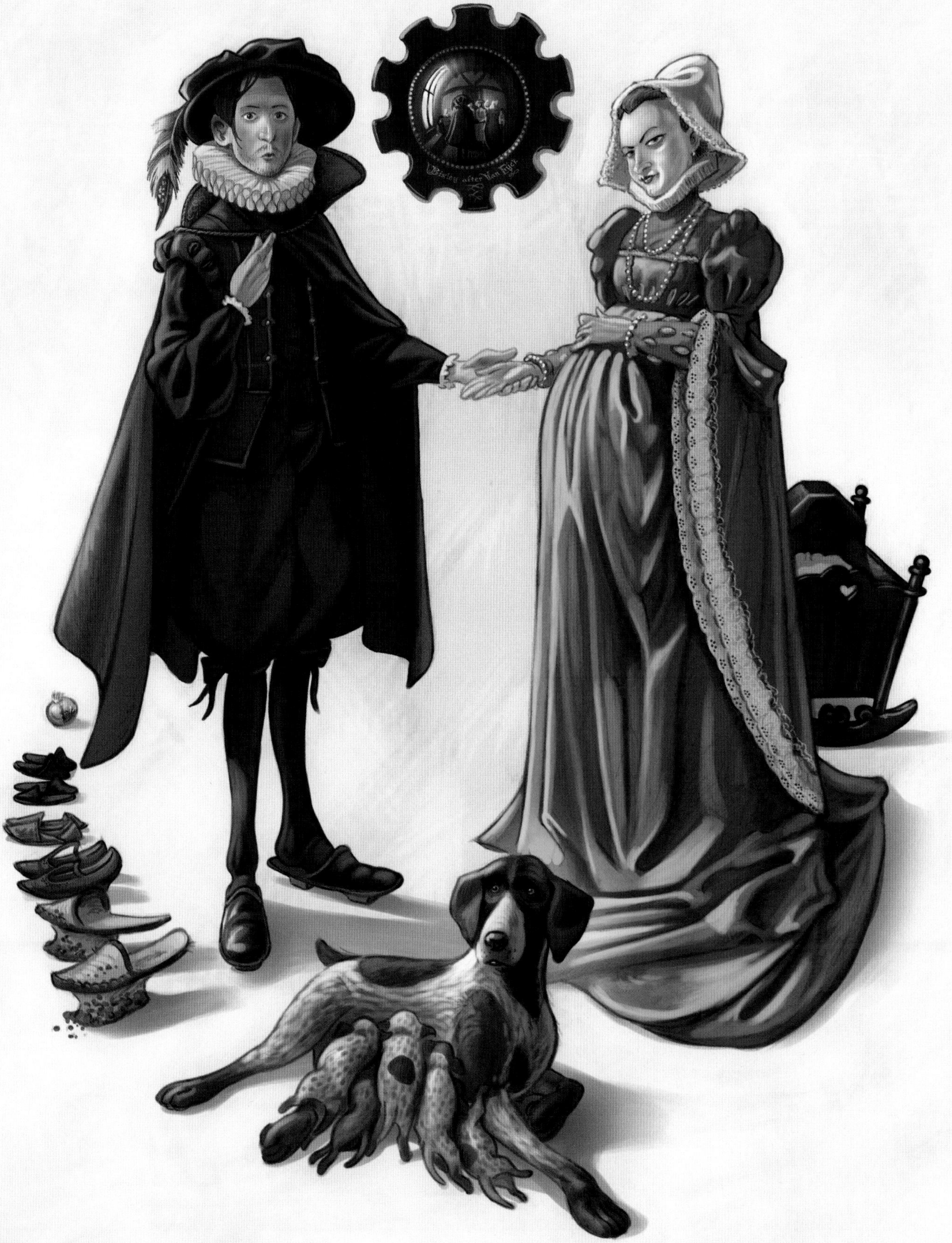
Bixley after Van Eyck

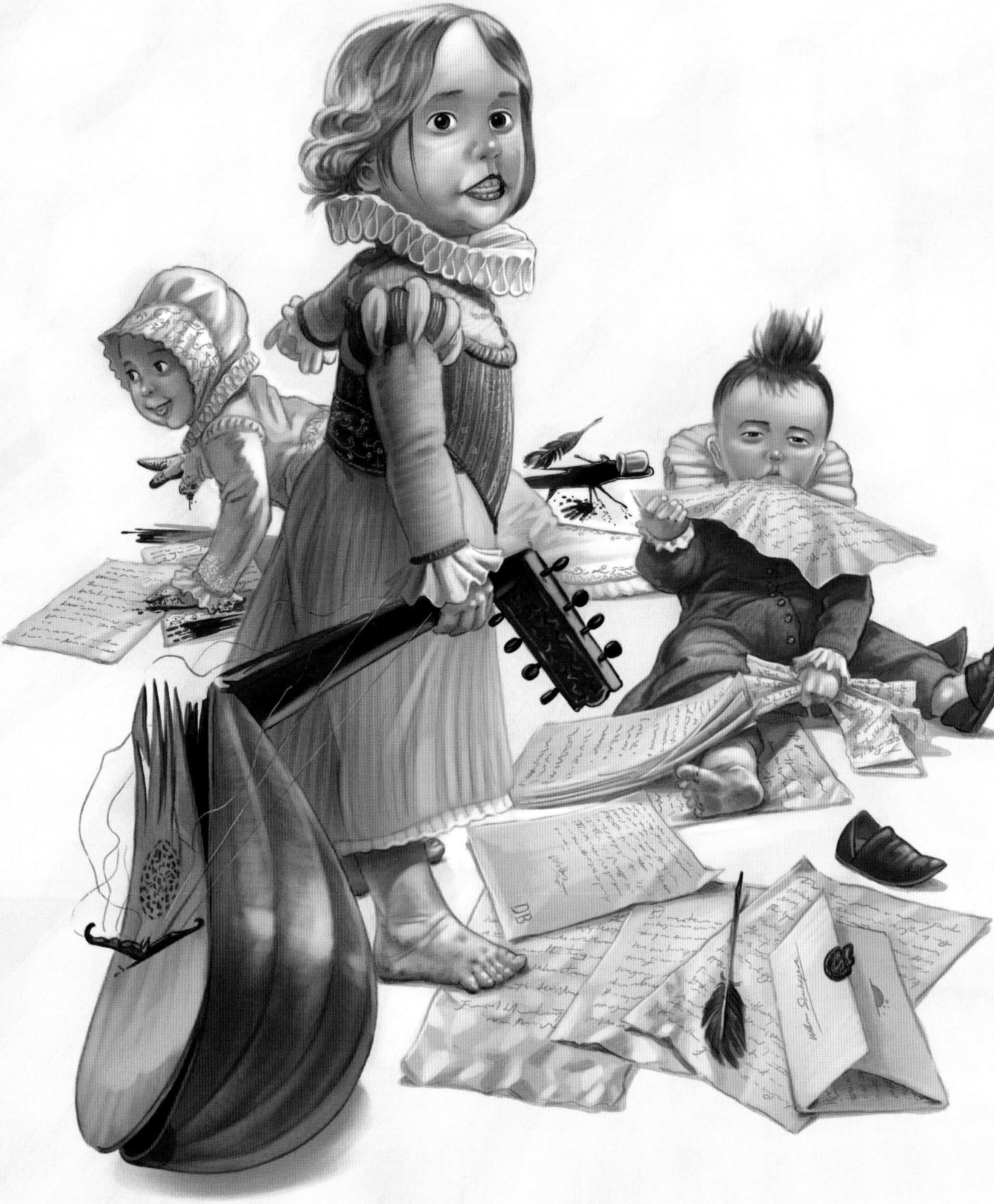

Double, double, toil and trouble.

MACBETH

Will and Anne's first child, Susanna, was born six months after the wedding in May 1583. She was followed two years later, in February 1585, with the birth of twins Hamnet and Judith. Will later included the confusion and mix-ups of twins in his plays *The Comedy of Errors* and *Twelfth Night*.

There is much speculation as to whether Anne had complications with the birth, as the couple had no more children.

We are such stuff as dreams are made on.

THE TEMPEST

Will would have adored the many acting troupes which passed through Stratford. But the players were often treated no better than vagrants. So, to avoid being whipped out of town with the 'sturdy beggars', acting troupes would seek the patronage and good name of a great lord. Hence in Will's life we encounter troupes such as the Lord Strange's Men, the Admiral's Men or the Chamberlain's Men.

At some point in his early twenties, Will decided to follow his dream of becoming a player and venturing out onto that world stage. It is quite likely that his ticket to London was joining a passing troupe of actors. It just happens that in 1587 the most famous troupe in the land, the Queen's Men, passed through Stratford and were one player down. But what of Will's wife and children? Well, he never abandoned them to penury, so it can be assumed that he left with a plan, or at least a promise, of employment.

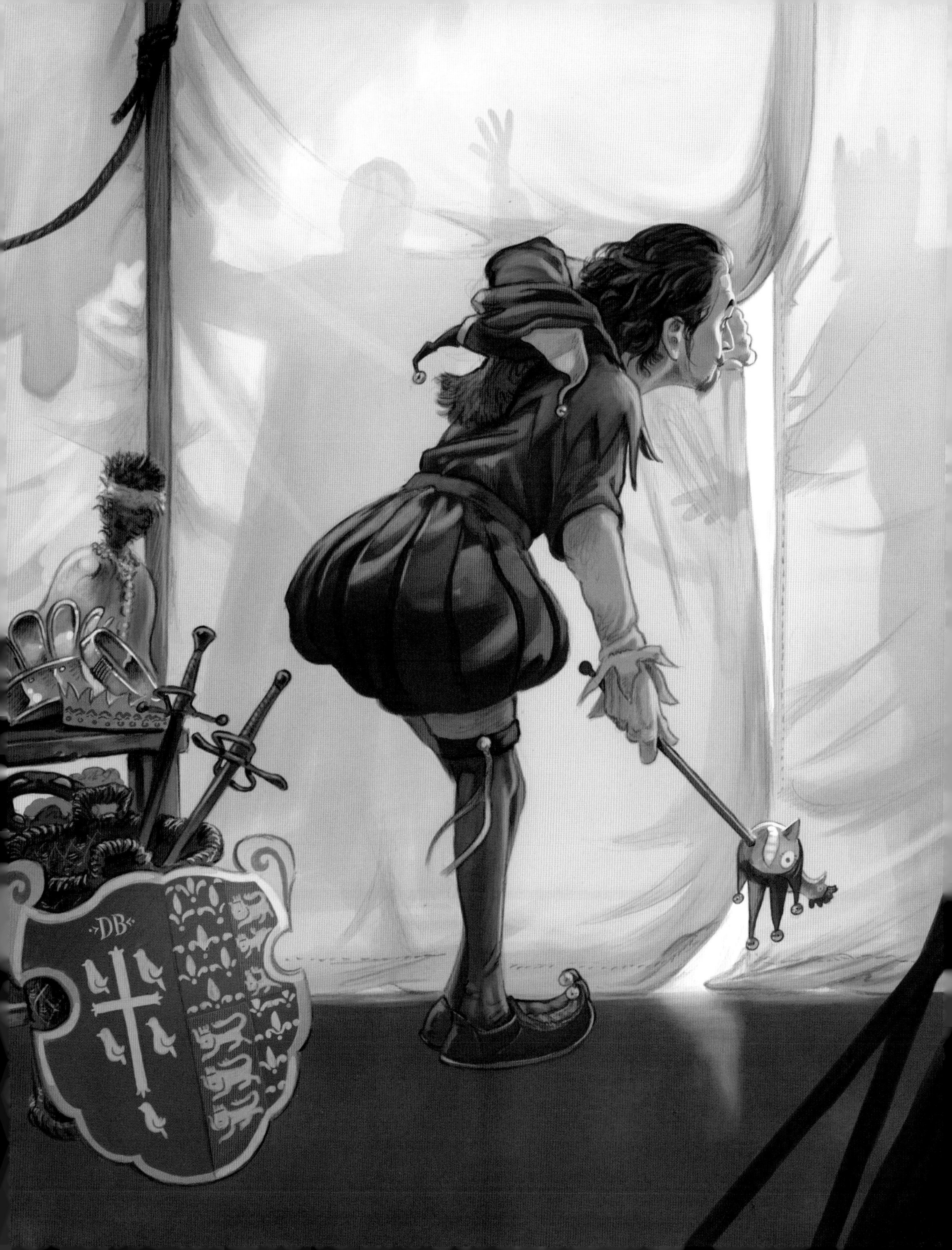
DB

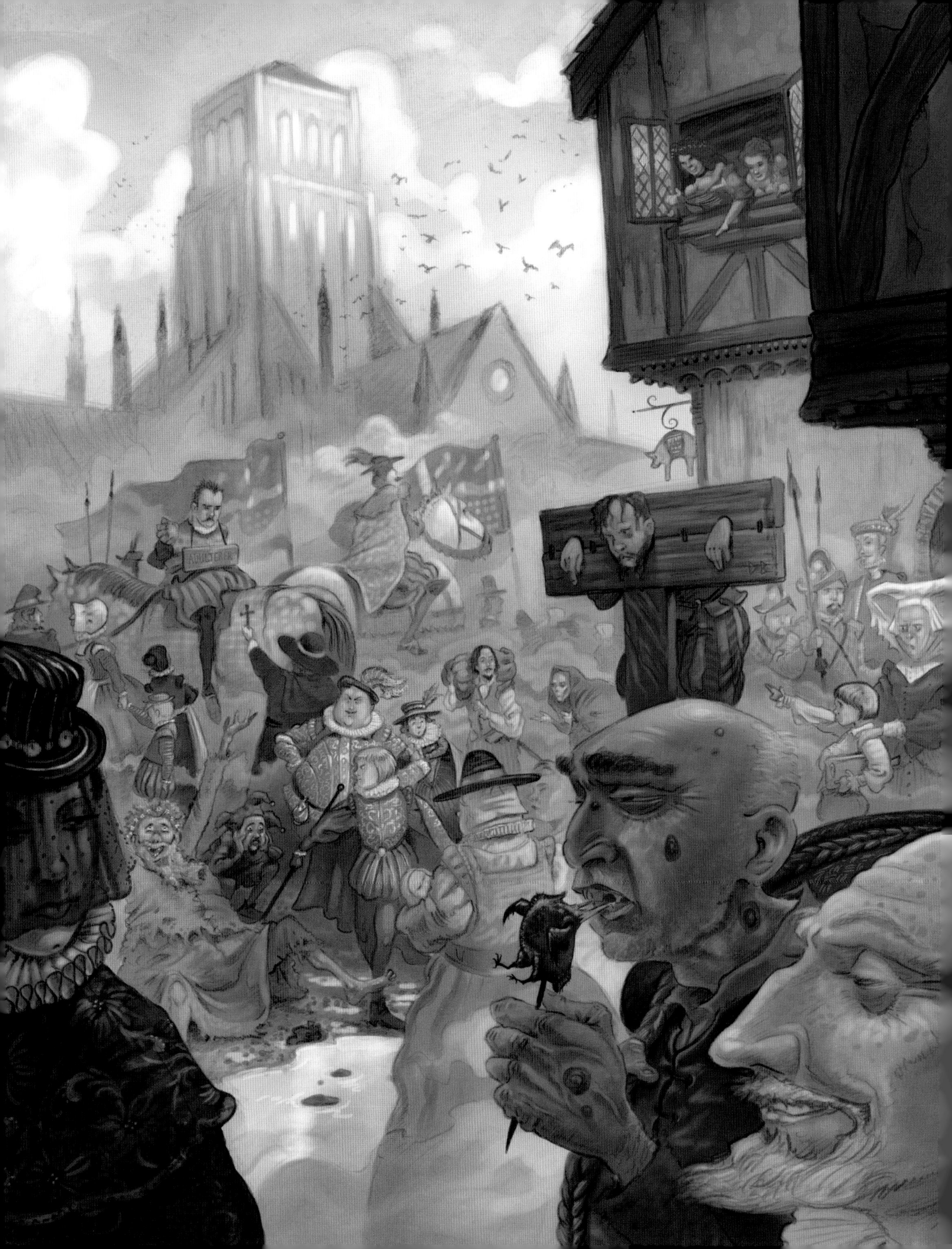

Fair is foul, and foul is fair: hover through the fog and filthy air.

MACBETH

The stink of London was legendary and Will would have smelled the city twenty miles away. With a population of over 100,000, London was going through a period of tremendous growth and would double in size within fifteen years. Like anyone entering the great city for the first time, Will would have been struck by the stark contrasts of fair and foul: the powerful courtiers parading their wealth, the extravagant pageants designed to keep the masses distracted, and the impressive structures of the city. On the other hand was the foul and filth of the open sewers and the tenements built on top of graveyards, where the working classes lived and the average life expectancy was only twenty-five. Will's fascination with juxtaposition and contrasts would become a signature of his plays.

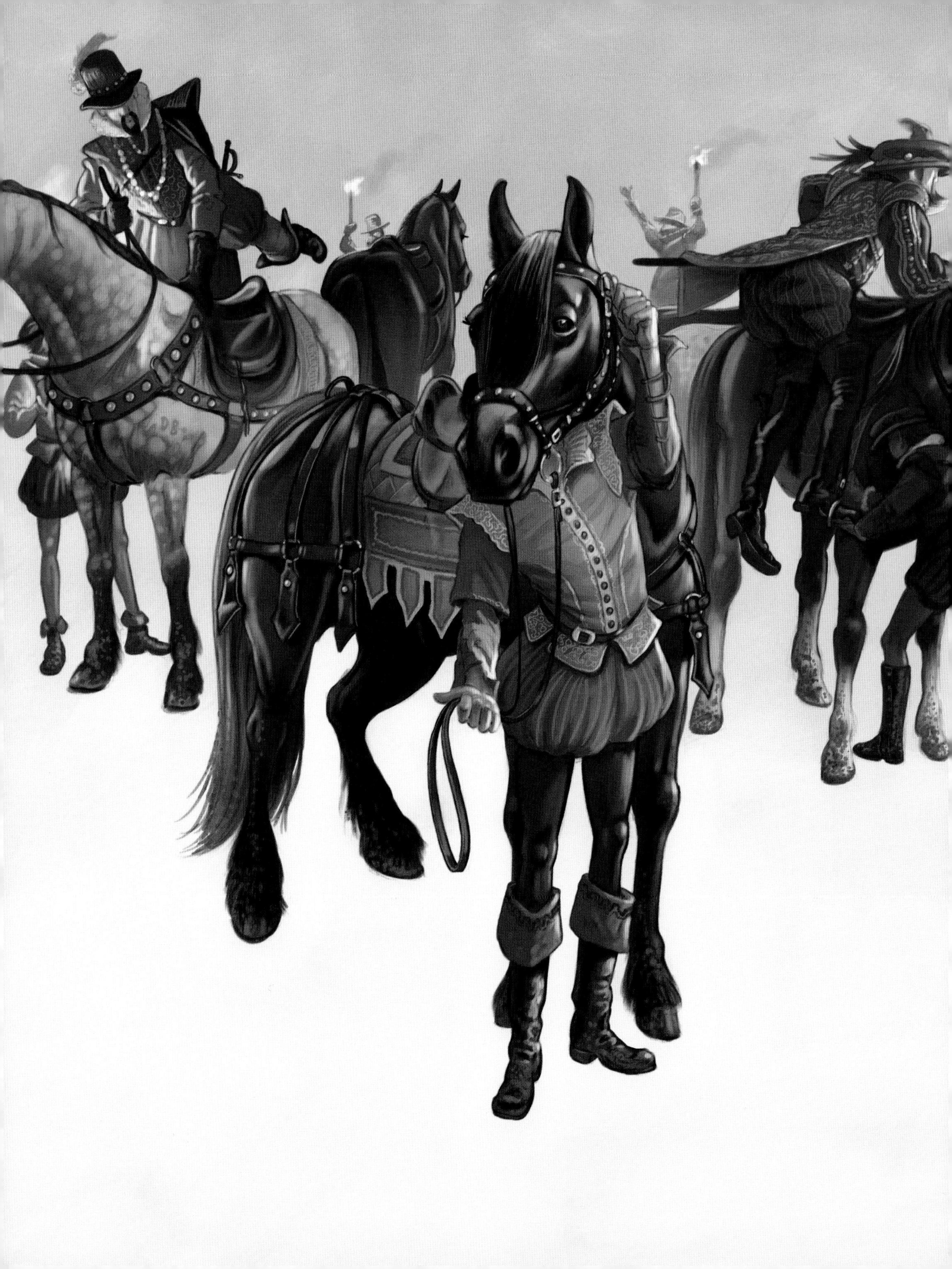

A horse! a horse! my kingdom for a horse!

RICHARD III

No one knows exactly what Will's prospects were in the big city or how he got his introduction to the theatre. One Shakespearean legend claims that he started at the bottom, as a horse-holder for wealthy patrons, moving up to call boy, prompter and eventually an actor. All of which seems a flimsy premise for Will to leave his family. Whatever the case, sometime in the mid to late 1580s Will arrived in the city and was soon acting in and contributing to plays.

As for the famous line, from Will's *Richard III* (written later in 1593), it was an instant classic amongst the theatre audiences and playwrights who parodied it in their own plays.

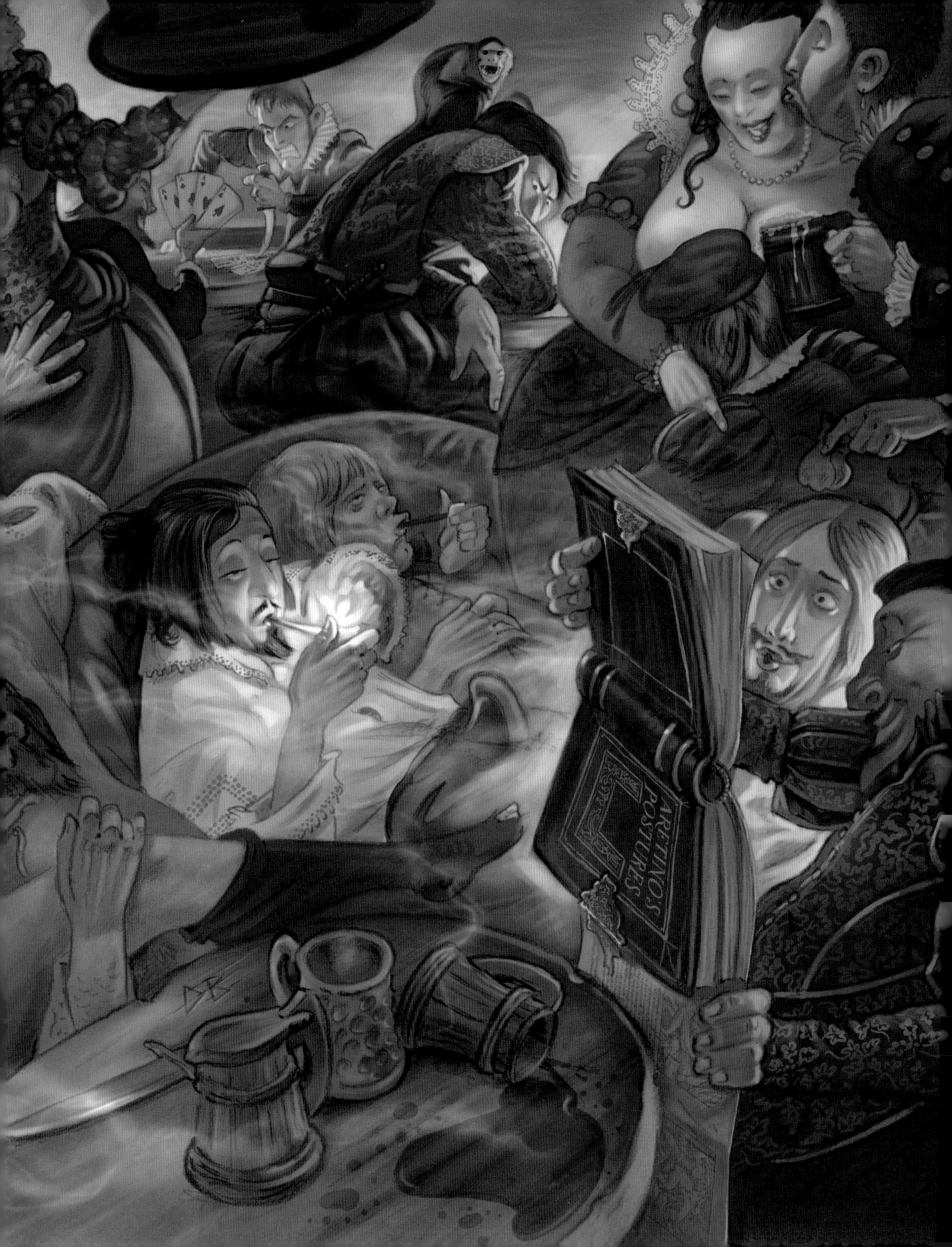
ARETINO'S POSTURES

Commit the oldest sins the newest kind of ways.

HENRY IV PART TWO

Brothels, gambling dens, animal fighting pits, taverns and playhouses — pretty much all the same thing as far as the Puritan authorities were concerned. These sinful businesses clustered together just outside the city's jurisdiction in the northern suburb of Shoreditch. This was Will's first London stomping ground, which he shared with many other actors and playwrights, who liked to live close to the theatres.

What an eye-opener for a lad from the country! Off-duty soldiers, half naked and fully drunk, searching for one of the trendy new taverns, where topless waitresses served ale or cannabis, and everyone had a copy of Aretino's *Postures* (the newly printed Italian pornography). Considering that he spent most of his life in such locations, away from his family, it's hard to imagine that a sexy young actor like Will didn't go a bit wild every now and then, even with the dire threat of venereal diseases.

Take arms against a sea of troubles.

HAMLET

The summer of 1588 was a do-or-die moment in England's history. The nation was readying for a desperate defence against the dreaded Spanish Armada. This occurred during Will's 'lost years' where there is no trace of him in any records. However, every male Londoner between seven and sixty had been conscripted for the national emergency. Will's fellow playwright Ben Jonson fought in Flanders, and twenty-four-year-old Will could well have been one of the thousands of soldiers and sailors enlisted — especially considering that actors were professionally trained in sword-craft.

Fortune was on England's side and it was the Spanish who had to sink or swim. After several uneventful skirmishes with the English navy, they were thrown into disarray by Sir Francis Drake's famous fire ships. In the event, a fierce storm blew the Armada up into the North Sea, where almost half the fleet sank or came to grief on the Scottish and Irish coasts as they straggled home via the North Atlantic. But there still remained the threat of a second Spanish force crossing from Dunkirk, so Queen Elizabeth, in grand theatrical style, turned up at Tilbury on the Firth of Thames, where she rode amongst the troops without her bodyguard, firing up the English defenders.

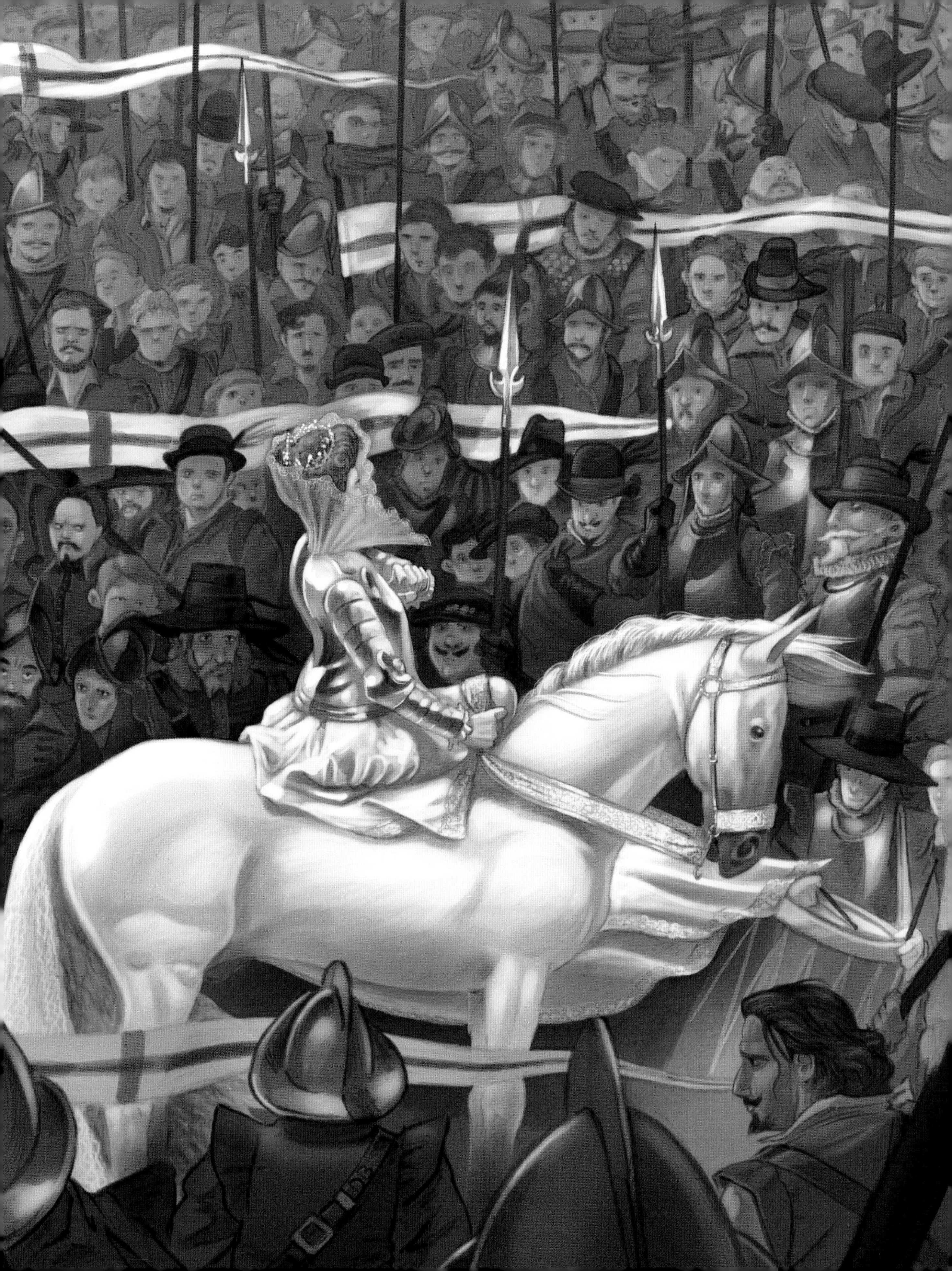

George Bryan

Henry Condell

Marlowe

Thomas Pope

We few, we happy few, we band of brothers.

HENRY V

By the end of 1588 Will was living the dream. He'd found his band of brothers and was acting and writing as a hired player with the Lord Strange's Men, many of whom would become his lifelong friends, workmates and rivals. Will's initial writings were collaborative, cobbled together from various sources by the whole troupe. The university-educated playwrights criticised him for being 'unlearned', but Shakespeare developed his writing skills first hand, as an actor on stage. In this way he was unique amongst Elizabethan playwrights. Will himself became renowned for playing kingly and authoritative roles including the ghost of Hamlet's father.

John Henninges

William Slye

Augustine Phillips

Richard Burbage

In such a pickle.

THE TEMPEST

In 1589 the Lord Mayor of London had to deal with those pesky actors yet again. This time they were performing plays that he had expressly banned — plays with a farcical religious content. The two main theatre troupes were called in and fairly warned, and whilst the Admiral's Men desisted, the Lord Strange's Men contemptuously continued to perform. Will was one of Lord Strange's players, and the troupe were quickly rounded up and thrown in gaol. What a pickle. The authorities were always keen to set an example for the masses, with torture and execution being standard procedure — even for what we would consider minor offences.

But that I am forbid to tell the secrets
of my prison-house, I could a tale unfold
whose lightest word would harrow up thy
soul, freeze thy young blood, make thy two
eyes, like stars, start from their spheres,
thy knotted and combined locks to part,
and each particular hair to stand on end
like quills upon the fretful porpentine.

HAMLET

In 1589 members of Will's troupe, the Lord Strange's Men, were imprisoned for performing banned plays. The prison house was a place from which you may never return or, indeed, may return but never whole again. Whipping was not uncommon, nor was being pilloried (having your ears nailed to a post and cut off), and being racked would cripple you for life. If you were hanged, you would hope that friends and family would haul on your legs to make your passing quicker. You could also be boiled in lead, or drawn and quartered whilst still alive — but that was saved for serious crimes.

Luckily Will's troupe was released from prison without being put to torture or death. They simply moved outside the city jurisdiction and performed at the Curtain Theatre. But it wouldn't be the last time Will was in trouble with the law.

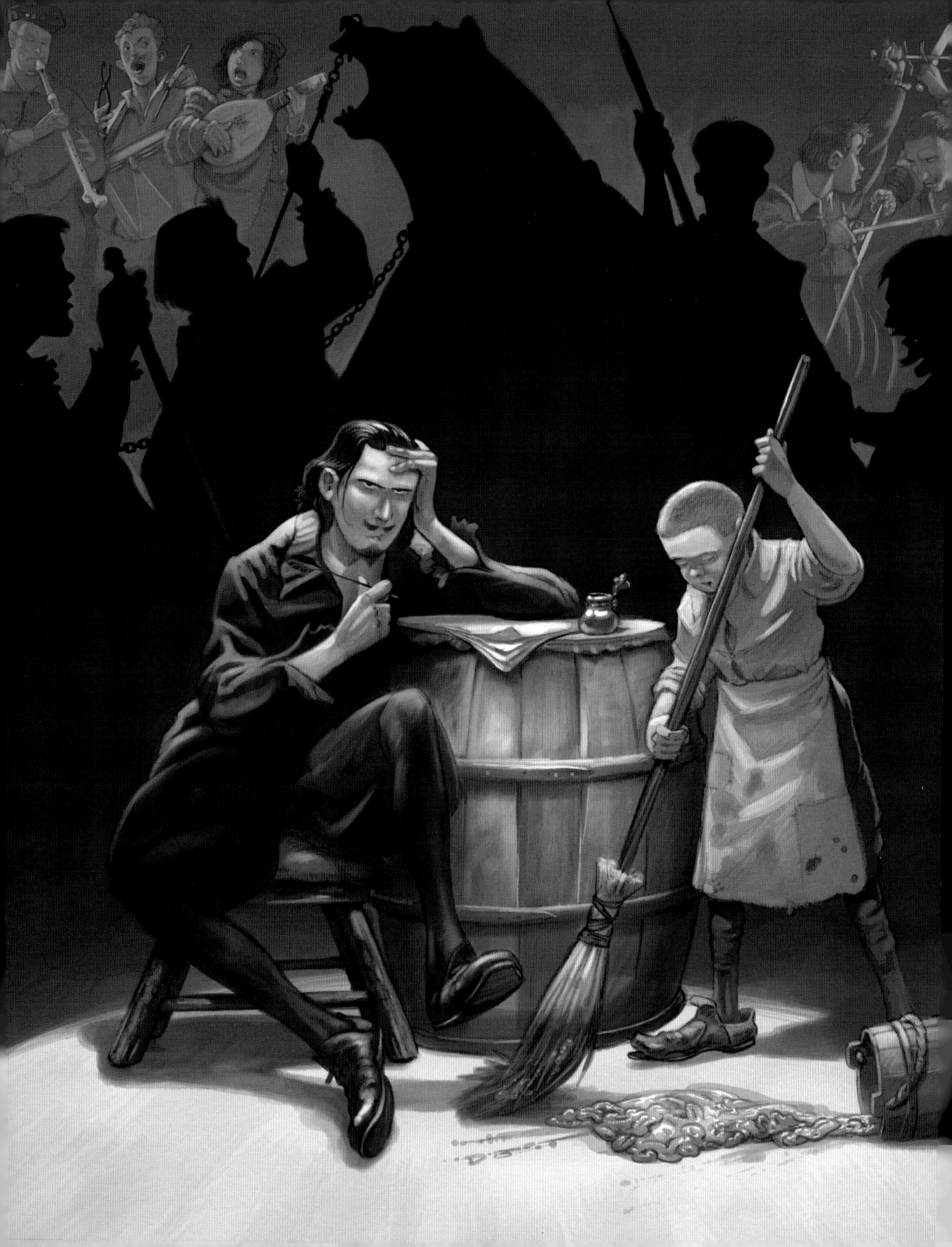

These are the youths that thunder at a playhouse.

KING HENRY VIII

In between morning rehearsals and the afternoon show, the young actors had training which included singing, acrobatics and wrestling. They also studied memory techniques, which were vital when you had up to thirty plays per season to remember! On top of this, actors were trained in knife and sword fighting at the fencing school. Their audiences would have expected a realistic performance as they saw real duels in the streets and bloody executions in daily life.

Shakespeare's plays contain all sorts of grisly props, such as fake eyeballs, severed heads, vials of blood and buckets of sheep guts. Even missing your cue could be life-threatening! 'Exit, pursued by a bear' is probably Shakespeare's most famous stage direction, from *The Winter's Tale* written at the end of his career. Very likely it involved a real bear from one of the popular bear-baiting pits nearby the playhouse. Within this storm of activity, it's amazing that Will could find time to write plays.

This blow might be the be-all and the end-all here.

MACBETH

It probably comes as no surprise to find that London's acting troupes were a volatile bunch of young drama queens. With their loud mouths, onstage swagger and sword training it's no surprise that they were keen to show off their fighting skills whenever a public brawl erupted, and many of Will's acting friends were killed, or killed others, in such fights. Theatrical types, such as Will's own leading man Richard Burbage, were constantly in trouble over all manner of minor dramas, many of which ended in acts of deadly violence. The playwright Ben Jonson, Will's off-and-on rival, famously had his thumb branded 'T' for Tyburn, the place where he would be hanged if he was caught at it again . . . as if that was going to stop him! All was well, if you could get away with it. Like any testosterone-fuelled young men, Will and his fellow actors thought they were bullet-proof, sword-proof and axe-proof.

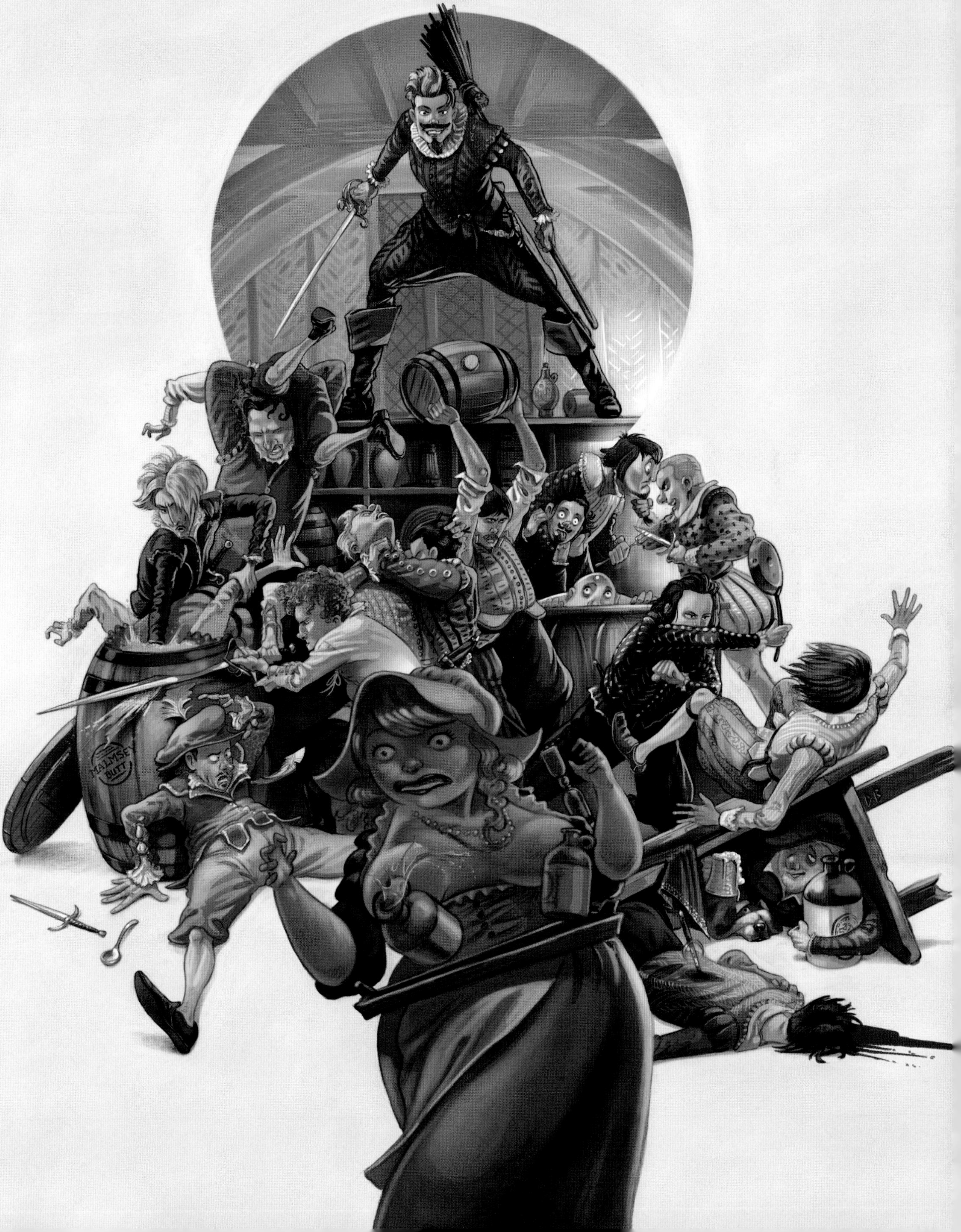
MALMSEY
BUTT

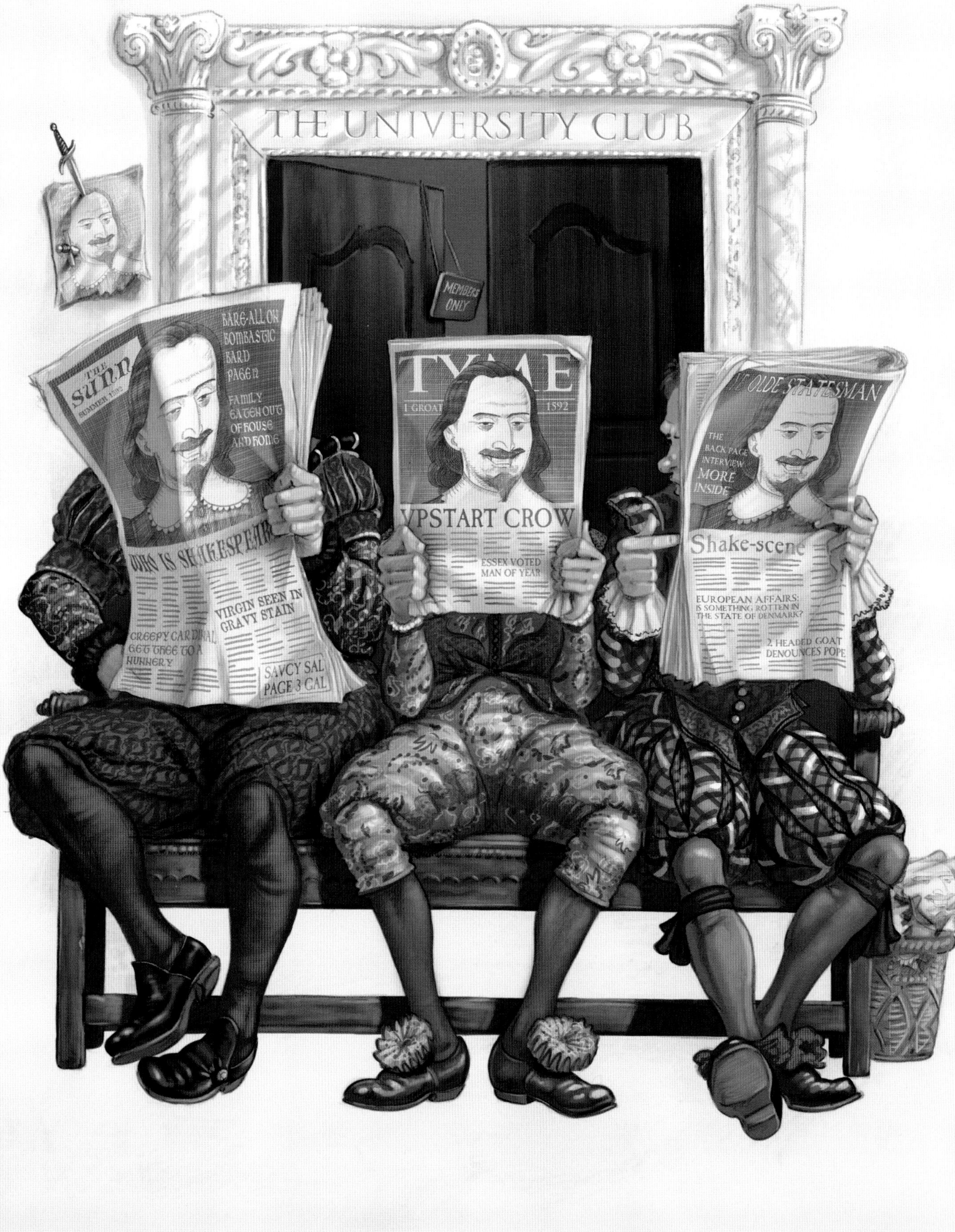
THE UNIVERSITY CLUB
MEMBERS ONLY
THE SUNN
SUMMER 1592
BARE-ALL ON BOMBASTIC BARD PAGE 12
FAMILY EATEN OUT OF HOUSE AND HOME
WHO IS SHAKESPEARE
VIRGIN SEEN IN GRAVY STAIN
CREEPY CARDINAL GET THEE TO A NUNNERY
SAVCY SAL PAGE 3 GAL
TYME
1 GROAT
1592
VPSTART CROW
ESSEX VOTED MAN OF YEAR
YE OLDE STATESMAN
THE BACK PAGE INTERVIEW
MORE INSIDE
Shake-scene
EUROPEAN AFFAIRS: IS SOMETHING ROTTEN IN THE STATE OF DENMARK?
2 HEADED GOAT DENOUNCES POPE

O, beware, my lord, of jealousy; it is the green-eyed monster which doth mock the meat it feeds on.

OTHELLO

An ambitious guy like Will would have coveted the success and education of his wealthy university rivals. But, in turn, they were jealous of the country boy and his fast-rising star. In 1592 came a slanderous pamphlet in which an older playwright, Robert Greene, criticised Shakespeare as a plagiarising 'upstart crow', a jack of all trades, and (possibly worst of all) an actor who fancied himself as a writer! When Greene called the young upstart 'beautified by our feathers', he was making fun of Shakespeare's habit of inventing words — one of them being 'beautified'. In a period when publishing was dominated by Latin, Will added over 2000 new words to written English (600 of them from *Hamlet* alone). Not long after Greene's attack, the publisher printed an apology to Will, indicating that William Shakespeare was already a writer of some respect. Indeed, he had much to be envied.

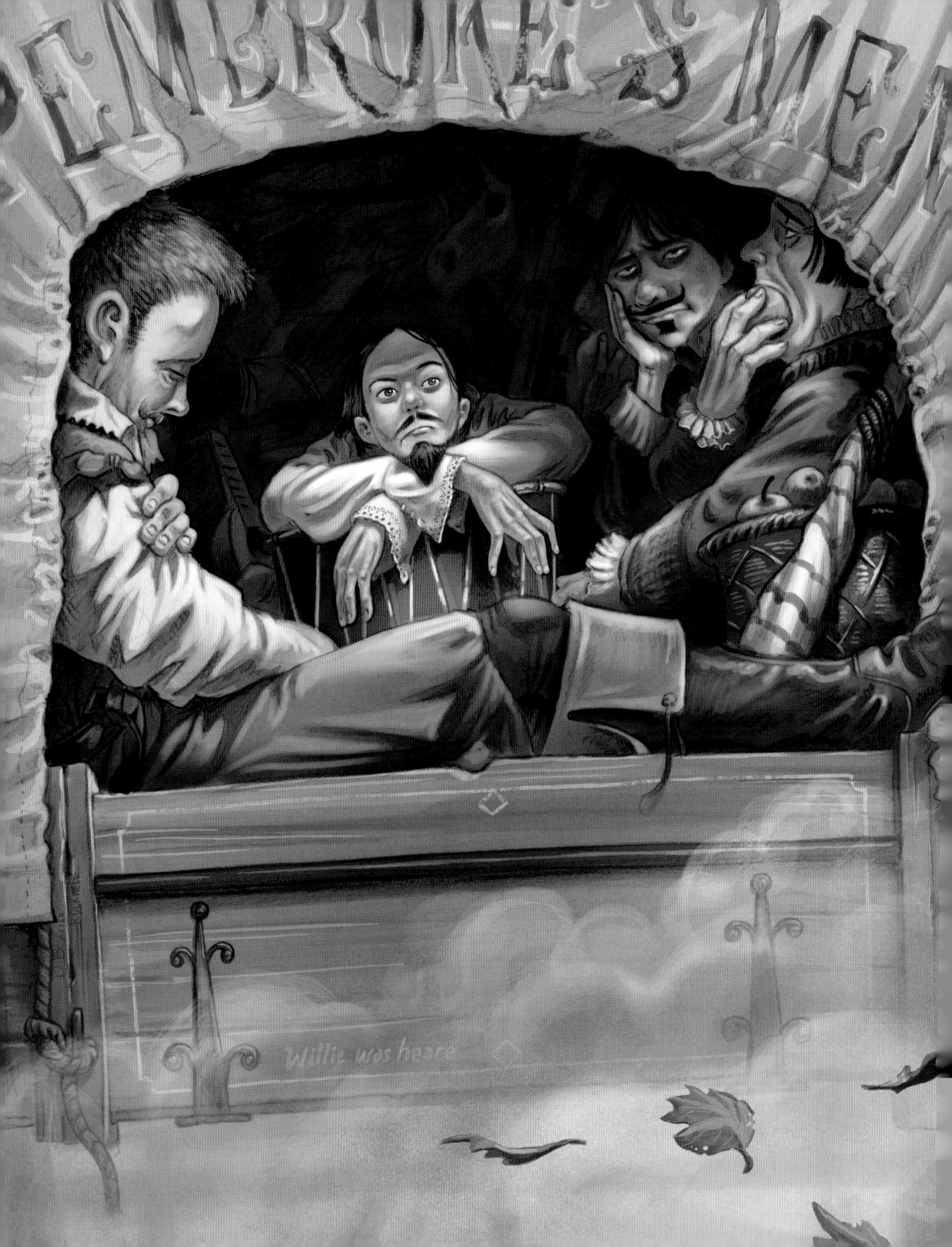
EMBROKE'S ME
Willie was heare

A plague o' both your houses!

ROMEO AND JULIET

In 1593 the constant rivalry between theatre troupes was put on hold by the plague. During most summers the theatres were periodically closed to prevent the spread of contagion, but in that year the plague struck with particular ferocity. Not only was it a threat to the lives of Londoners but also to the livelihood of players. To earn a living, Will's current troupe (the Lord Pembroke's Men) toured the countryside for eighteen months, eventually having to disband because of bankruptcy. In Will's early plays the plague is used in a metaphorical sense. However, in his life the plague struck London again in 1603 and 1608. The 1603 terror carried off 38,000 people, including two of Will's fellow actors. In his later works the plague becomes a real and sinister presence.

The slings and arrows
of outrageous fortune.

HAMLET

The closure of theatres must have hit Will hard. Here he was, champing to prove his mettle, only to have his main livelihood taken away. The alternative turned out to be a blessing in disguise. In 1593, to make a bit of cash, he wrote the long narrative poem *Venus and Adonis* and dedicated it to the Earl of Southampton. It was sold at the bookstalls outside St Paul's and was the first time Shakespeare's name appeared as author. *Venus and Adonis* was a voluptuous love poem in which Cupid's arrows bordered on pornographic . . . well, for Elizabethan times, that is. It was an instant hit (not the last time a risqué publication proved popular) and everyone read it. Even the university snobs admired Will, and his poem became one of the most successful publications of the era. What outrageous highs and lows. In one year Will had gone from 'upstart crow' to the most famous writer in England. Soon he began introducing those sumptuous poetic speeches into his plays.

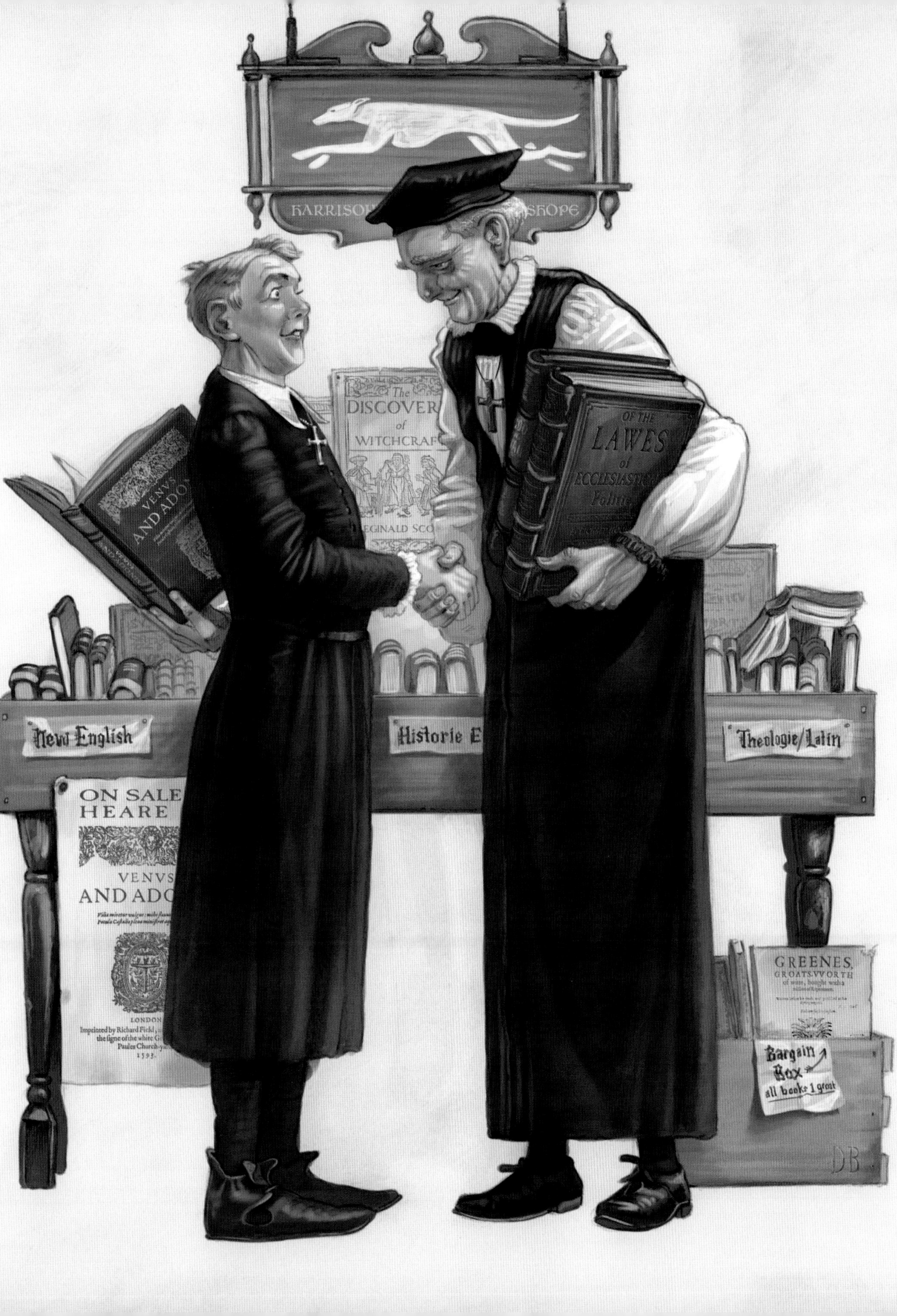
HARRISO
SHOPE
The
DISCOVER
of
WITCHCRAF
EGINALD SCO
VENVS
AND ADO
OF THE
LAWES
of
ECCLESIASTI
New English
Historie E
Theologie/Latin
ON SALE
HEARE
VENVS
AND ADO
LONDON
Imprinted by Richard Field,
the signe of the white G
Paules Church-ya
1593.
GREENES
GROATS-VVORTH
Bargain
Box
all books 1 groat
DB

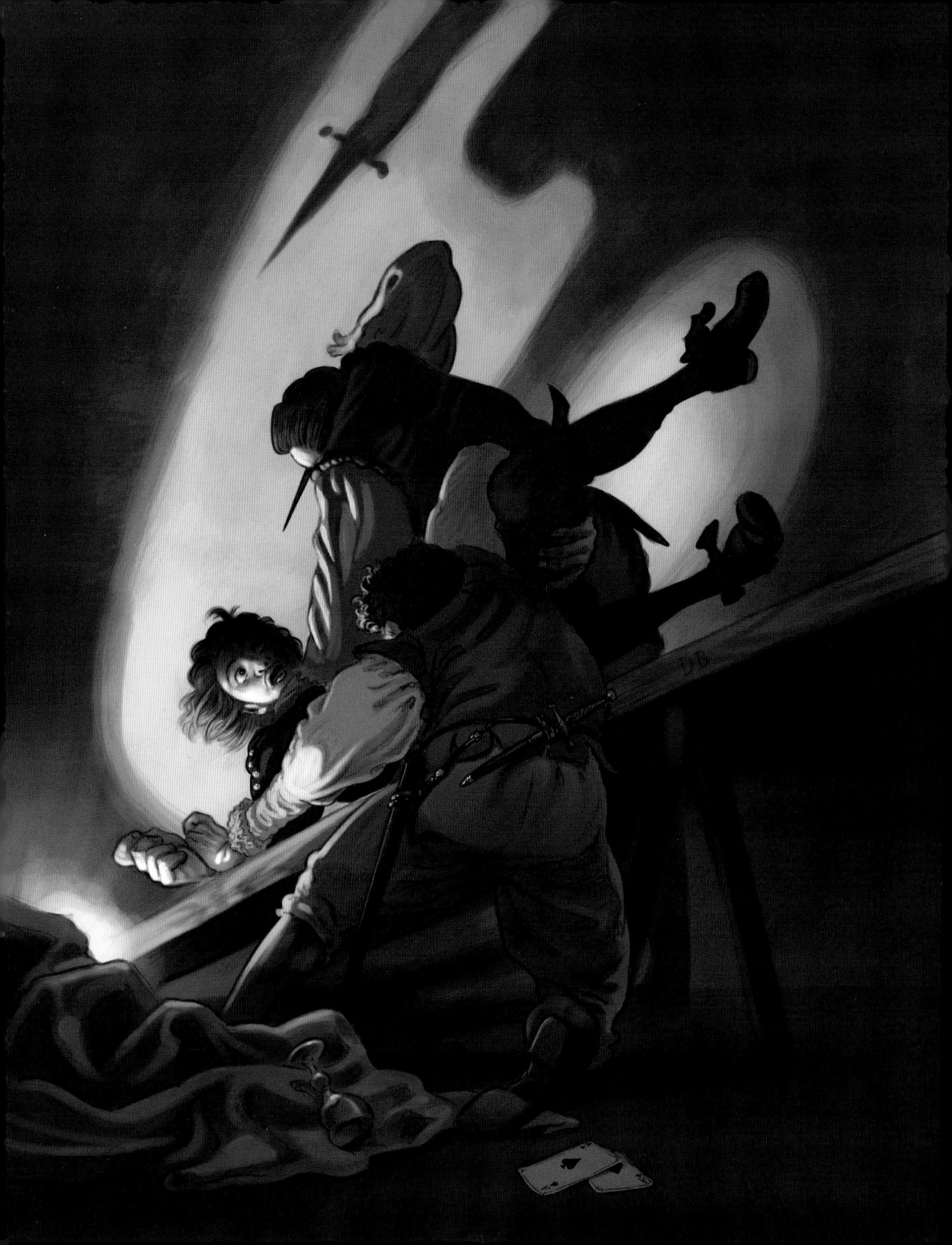

Out, vile jelly!

KING LEAR

Will's early plays imitate his university-educated rival, the mysterious Christopher Marlowe (who was also rumoured to moonlight as a spy). In 1593 Will and Marlowe were both twenty-nine, and up until then it was Marlowe who was the superior playwright. In that fateful year, however, the hot-headed Marlowe was murdered during a brawl over a bill with a fellow spy. He was stabbed in the eye with his own dagger. That same year, a second senior playwright, Thomas Kyd, was imprisoned for inciting xenophobic riots. He was brutally tortured and eventually died the following year, leaving Will as London's supreme playwright. But he was still in Marlowe's shadow.

In the immediate years following Marlowe's death, Will managed to shrug off the influence of his larger-than-life contemporary, surpassing Marlowe with his early masterpieces *Romeo and Juliet*, *Richard III* and *A Midsummer Night's Dream*.

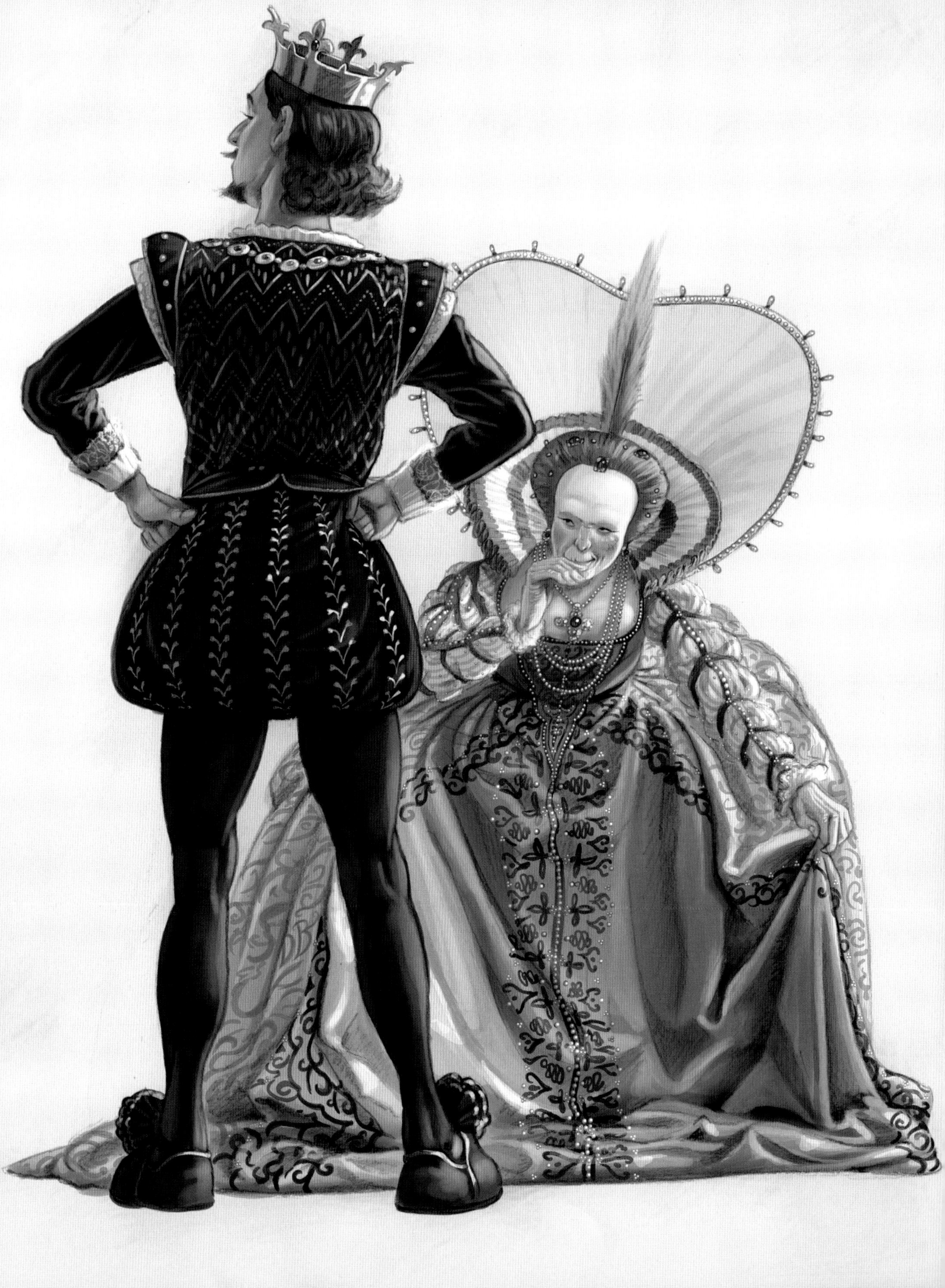

Some are born great, some achieve greatness, and some have greatness thrust upon 'em.

TWELFTH NIGHT

The huge demand for new plays meant that works such as *Romeo and Juliet* were churned out in a frenzy of creative genius, taking only two or three weeks! Will's main concern was the creation of great entertainment, not where he got his ideas from. This often led to cries of plagiarism from his contemporaries. But Will was taking plays to new heights — and this was an art form which had barely been legal a decade beforehand. In 1594 Will became a 'sharer' or partner in the Lord Chamberlain's Men. For his investment of £50 (the price of an expensive house in the country) he could now benefit directly from the troupe's financial success. In that same year the Chamberlain's Men performed for the Queen. An outrageous anecdote from the eighteenth century has Will playing a king and Elizabeth playfully bowing before him. According to the story, Will cheekily stayed in character, ignoring the queen and continuing his performance without missing a beat.

That which we call a rose by any other name would smell as sweet.

ROMEO AND JULIET

But a woman on stage, by any other name, was a man. Puritan authorities viewed the theatre as an evil lure away from the church. Plays, actors and even the actual playhouses were deemed so immoral that during some periods women were banned from the audience, never mind actually performing on stage. Nevertheless Will created some of the most memorable and complex female roles, all of which were performed by young men. It wasn't until 1629 — thirteen years after Will's death — that the first woman appeared on the English stage. This first performer was booed and hissed from the theatre and it was another thirty years before female players were commonly accepted by audiences.

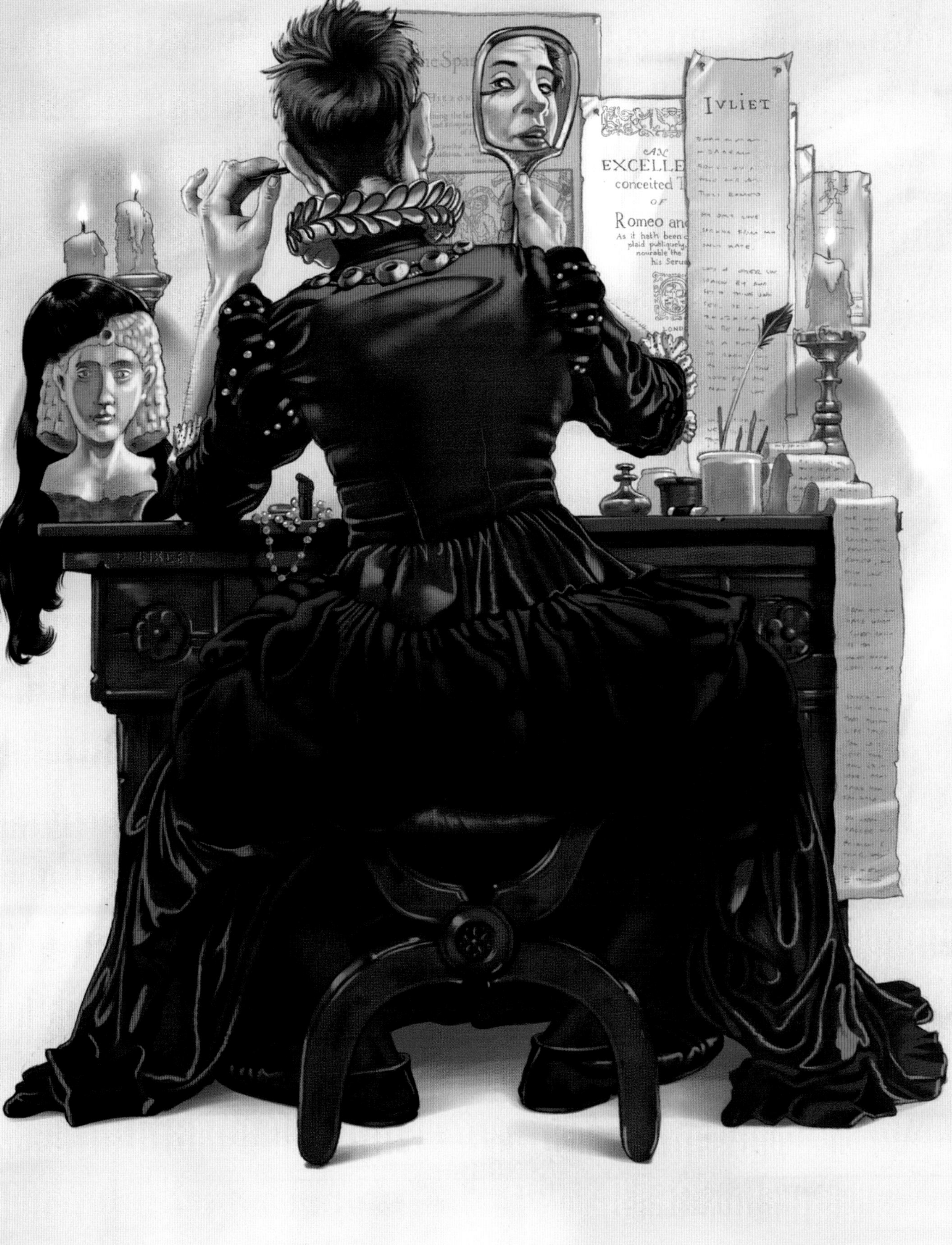
IVLIET
AN
EXCELLE
conceited T
OF
Romeo and
As it hath been
plaid publiquely,
nourable the
his Seruan

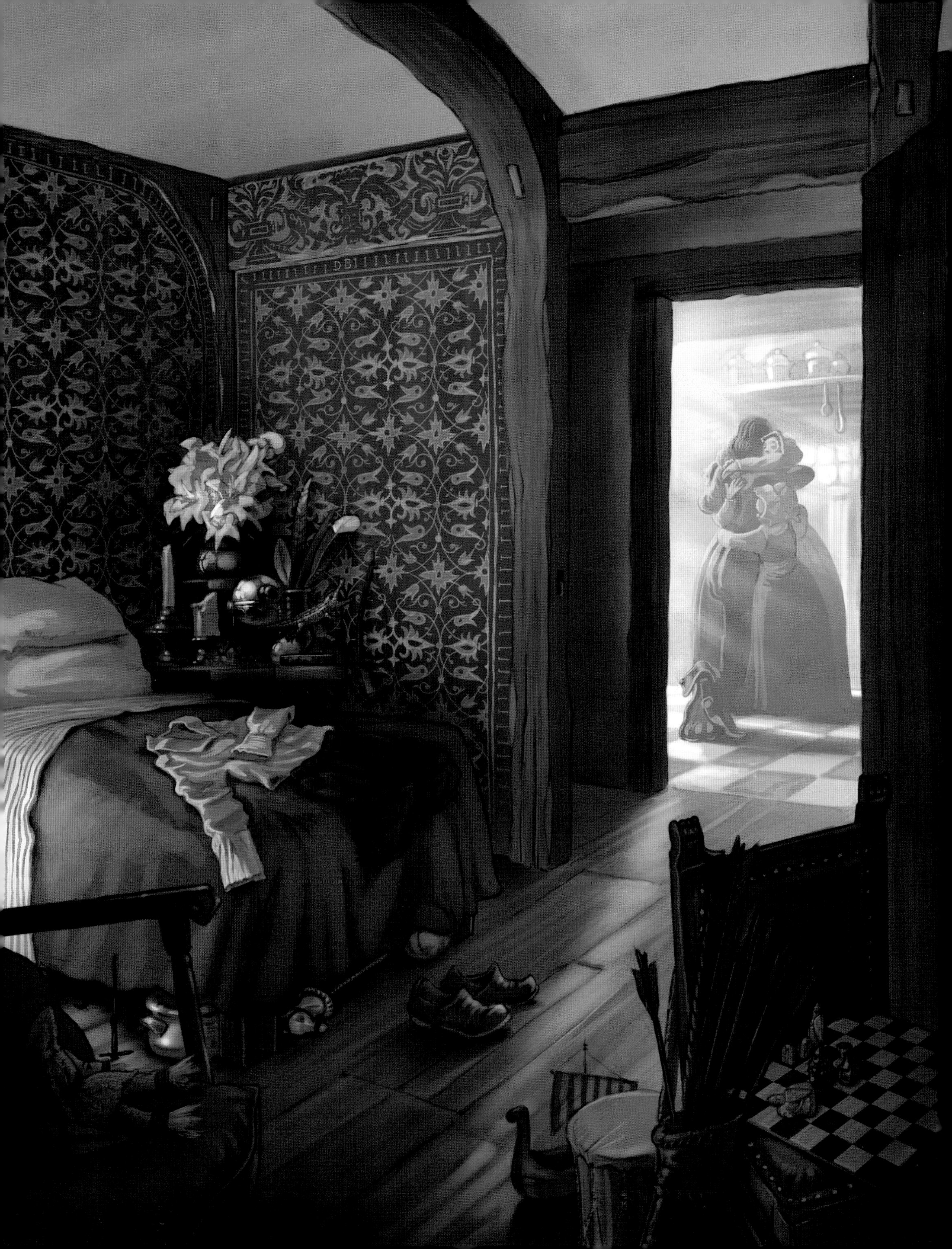

Grief fills the room up of my absent child,

lies in his bed, walks up and down with me,

puts on his pretty looks, repeats his words,

remembers me of all his gracious parts,

stuffs out his vacant garments with his form.

KING JOHN

Personal tragedy came to Will's doorstep in 1596 when his eleven-year-old son Hamnet died. The cause is not known, although many in Stratford that year died of typhus. It is not known how much contact Will had with his family back home, or how close he was to his son, but shortly after Hamnet's death Will updated his play *King John*, adding the above passage.

Later in the year Will helped win his father's twenty-year battle to be granted a coat of arms. Will could now claim gentility, but he no longer had a son to carry on his name.

Misery acquaints a man with strange bed-fellows.

THE TEMPEST

During his career Will wrote 154 sonnets, and there has probably been more speculation about them than any other work of literature. Like a great deal of Shakespeare's life, almost nothing can be said for certain about his sonnets. That hasn't stopped centuries of scholars claiming them to be a window into Will's personal world during the mid-1580s and 1590s. So what was he feeling after the death of Hamnet? Do they reveal a man in his thirties having a typical mid-life crisis? Is this what he got up to away from home? Will writes of an adulterous affair with a 'dark lady' as well as a passionate fling with a fair young man (much to the horror of many prudish historians). They were published as a complete set in 1609, but it is not known whether Will even authorised the printing.

THE ROSE

THE GLOBE

By the pricking of my thumbs, something wicked this way comes.

MACBETH

In the summer of 1596 Will was facing professional problems too. The troupe's protector, Henry Carey the Lord Chamberlain, died, leaving Shakespeare's company in a very uncertain position. England's first theatre had been built only twenty years beforehand and, in that time, the playhouses had come to be seen as Satan's snares. The Lord Mayor of London associated theatres with drunks and gamblers, horse-stealers, whore-mongers and practisers of treason (some of which was true). Now the new Lord Chamberlain, William Brooke, sided with the Lord Mayor and his Puritan wowsers. Together they made a concerted effort to close down the wicked playhouses once and for all, and Will was named in a legal action against one of the theatres. Luckily for all theatre lovers, the new Lord Chamberlain died and was replaced by Henry Carey's son. With George Carey as their patron, Shakespeare's company were reinstated in pride of place as the 'Lord Chamberlain's Men'.

Fashion wears out more apparel than the man.

MUCH ADO ABOUT NOTHING

Will was a hip young celebrity in the hottest city on the planet. With money burning a hole in his purse he could keep up with all the trendy gimmicks. Every other Londoner owned a parrot or a monkey, because that's what the biggest celebrity in the land had. However, Queen Liz had her own ideas about fashion. In 1597 she attempted to ban (for the umpteenth time) the wearing of fancy clothes by the common people, especially clothes sporting gold, silver, purple or velvet. After all, how was one to stand apart from the masses if everyone looked fabulous?

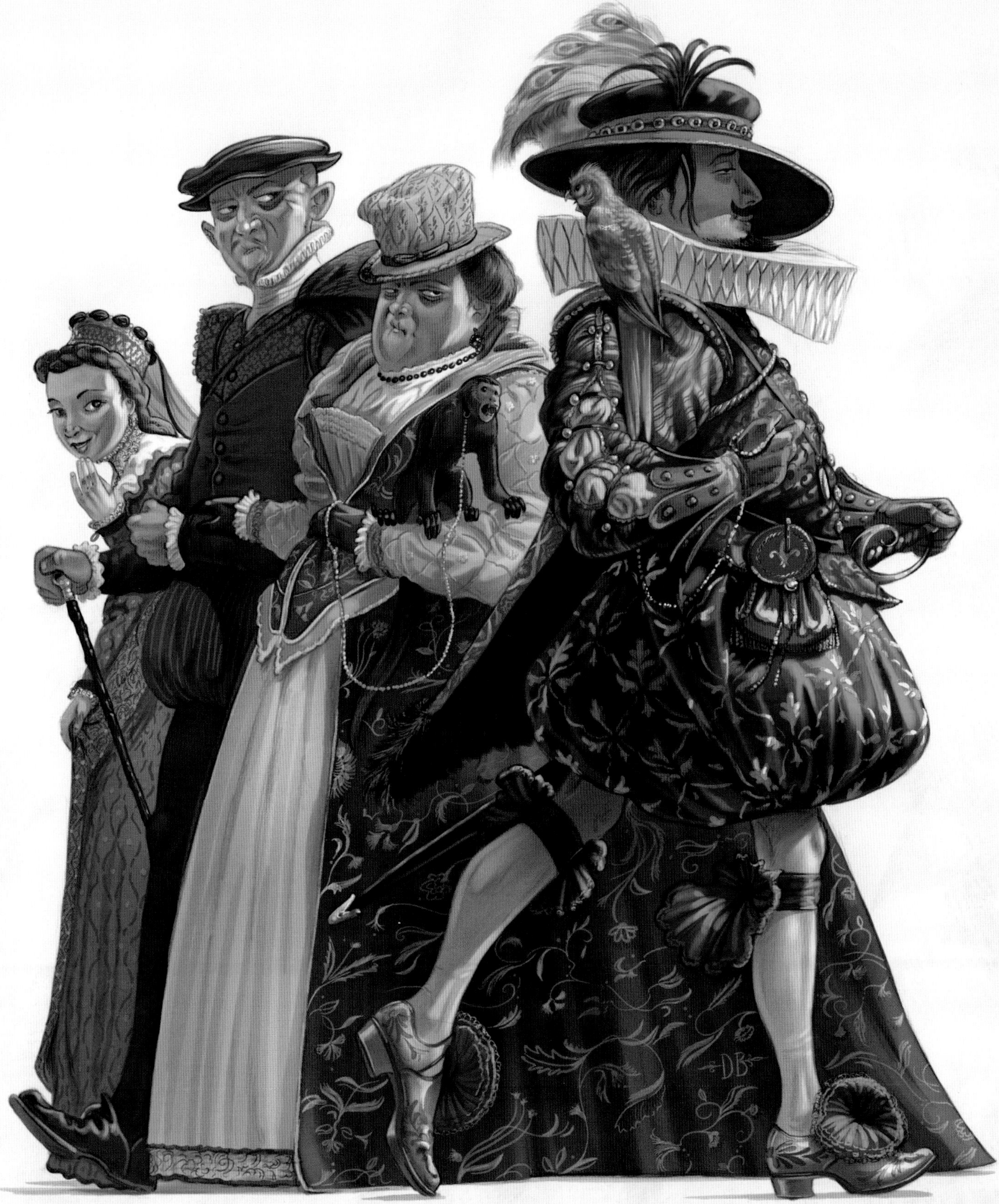

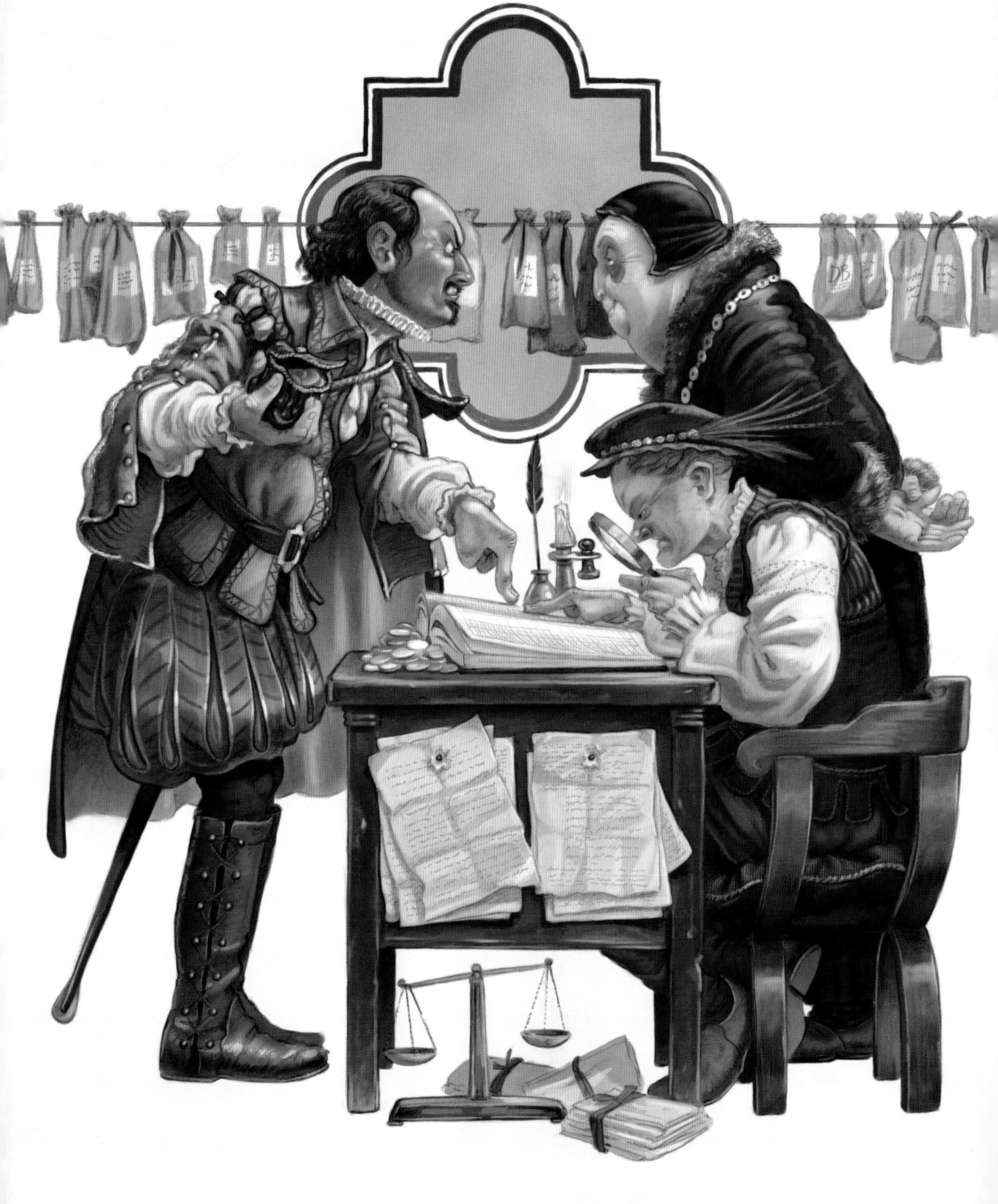

I can get no remedy against this consumption of the purse.

HENRY VI PART TWO

Despite living the bachelor life in London, Will didn't fritter away his new-found wealth. He proved himself to be an astute investor over the years, purchasing many properties in his home town of Stratford and one in London. In 1597 he had sufficient wealth to purchase New Place, the second largest house in Stratford, proof that he was the home-town boy done good. These appearances mattered to him and he was prudent in securing a legacy for his family and a comfortable retirement for himself. But increased income came hand in hand with that eternal and ever-present bleeder of the purse: taxes. In that same year Will was reported for not paying his share to the taxman, which became a regular event.

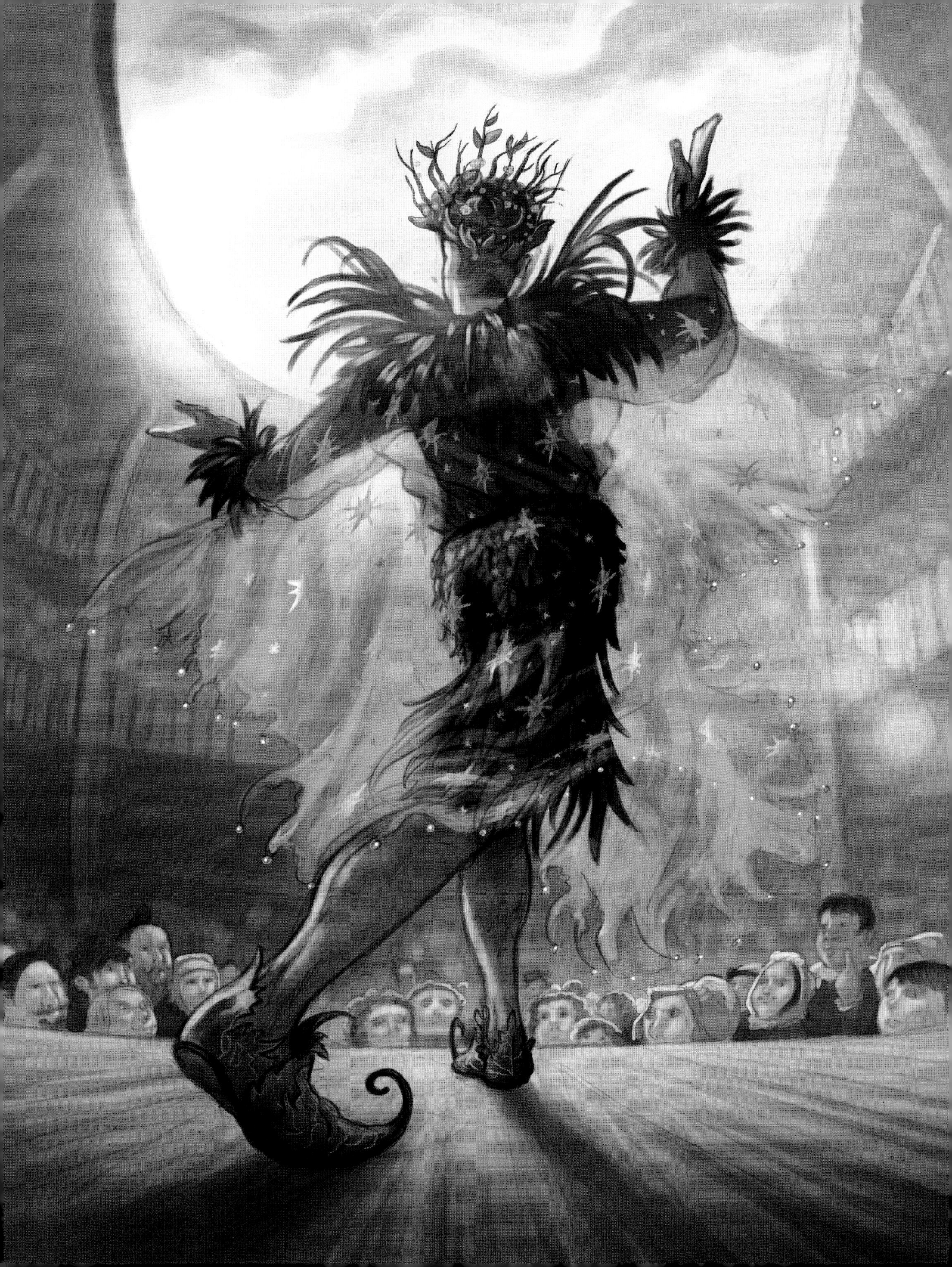

The purpose of playing . . . was and is, to hold, as 'twere, the mirror up to nature.

HAMLET

By 1598 Will's name as playwright was now a drawcard on its own, and he created roles specifically to suit the actors in his troupe. No longer was he just entertaining the crowds, but reflecting the heart of human nature. As the decade rolled on, comedy gave way to the popularity of new tragic roles. The actors expressed every emotion with a formal action, and the style of the time was to strut and fret about the stage, showing off your hamstrings, which gives us the term 'ham' acting. It was a grand and exaggerated performance which Elizabethans called 'tearing a cat upon the stage'. Richard Burbage was the leading actor of Will's troupe (as well as the nation) and he became renowned for a new naturalistic performance . . . well, 'natural' for Elizabethan times, that is. In response, Will wrote more subtle and complicated roles such as Othello, King Lear and Hamlet. Hamlet himself bemoans actors who 'saw the air too much with their hands' and 'tear a passion to tatters'.

What the dickens.

THE MERRY WIVES OF WINDSOR

In the winter of 1598 Will's troupe, the Lord Chamberlain's Men, were having a few unwelcome dramas with their playhouse, the Theatre. It seemed that the landlord owned the property, but not the actual building — this was owned by the troupe's leading man, Richard Burbage, and his brother. Naturally, there was only one thing to do! A few days after Christmas, Burbage and his colleagues took the unprecedented step of dismantling the Theatre. It was a most bitter winter and they carted it south, across the frozen Thames, to rebuild on a piece of land they had leased there. Of course the landlord was surprised, to say the least. In typical Elizabethan style the dismantling and transportation was conducted under a barrage of violent abuse and legal threats between the parties. The above exclamation has nothing to do with the writer Charles Dickens but is instead a bastardisation of 'what the Devil'.

Now is the winter
of our discontent,
made glorious summer . . .

RICHARD III

William, always on the lookout for new investment opportunities, decided to become a financial partner in the new venture. So when the glorious playhouse opened the next summer he would now share in the proceeds of both the troupe and the theatre.

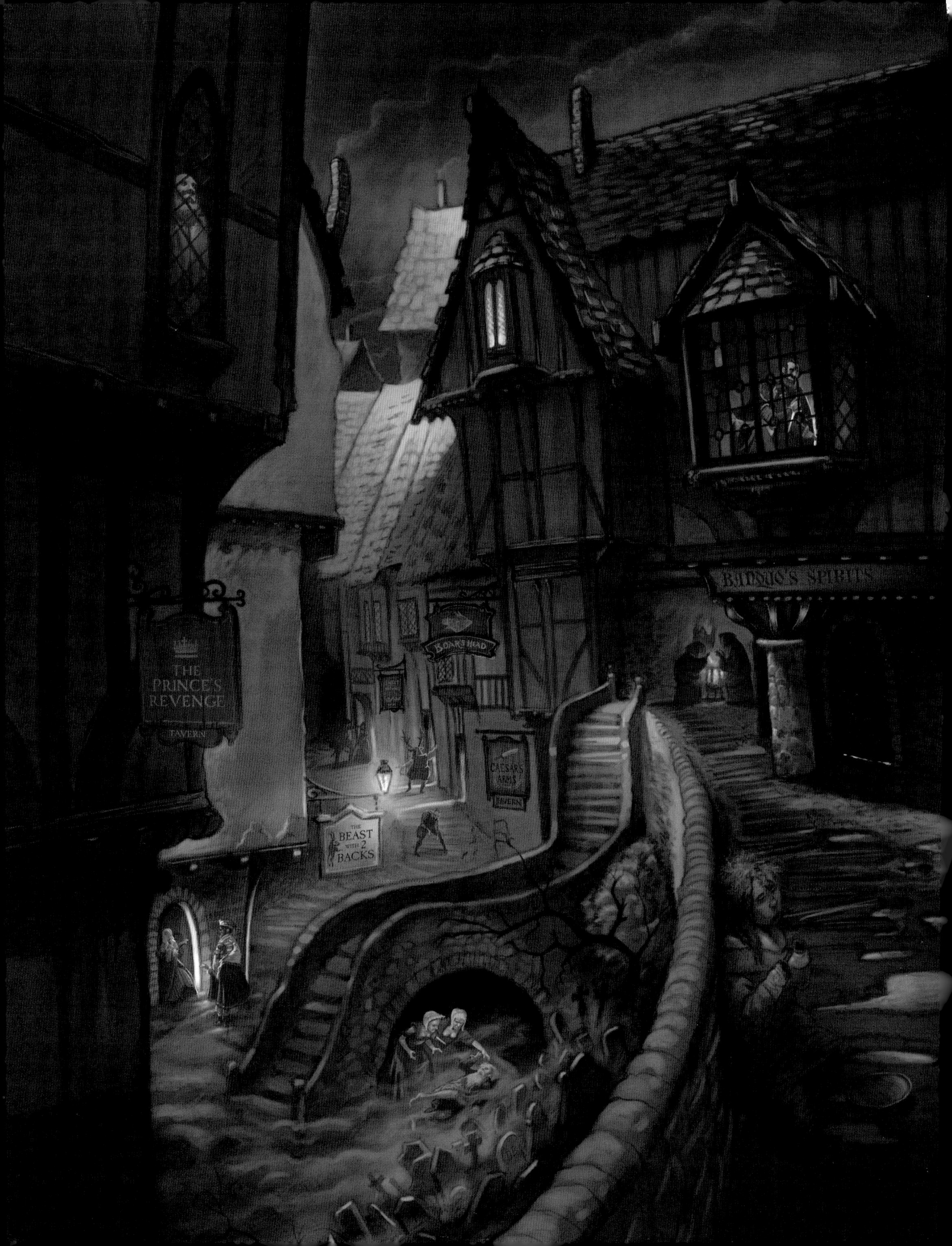
THE PRINCE'S REVENGE
TAVERN
BOAR'S HEAD
CAESAR'S ARMS
TAVERN
THE BEAST WITH 2 BACKS

'Tis now the very witching time of night, when churchyards yawn and hell itself breathes out contagion to this world.

HAMLET

Will sure lived in some insalubrious areas. Early in 1599 he moved to Southwark, on the southern side of the Thames, to be close to the new theatre. Petty thieves, con men, fortune tellers, prostitutes, cripples, immigrants and murderers — the characters who populate Will's plays all lived there.

Southwark was a contagious hell of desperate overcrowding. New tenements were built on top of old graveyards, sitting cheek by jowl with over 300 brothels and taverns, many of which were owned by the playhouse operators. From down the road came the constant noise of the hundreds of dogs which were unleashed on imported bears in the animal-baiting rings.

A most auspicious star, whose influence, if now I court not, but omit, my fortunes will ever after droop.

THE TEMPEST

It took only five months to reconstruct the Theatre, the impending opening of which was cause for much consulting of the stars. In a society that believed in witches and fairies, the consultation of stars was a serious profession. Palm reading, crystal waving, seeing signs in entrails or spinning tops was practised by the leading scientists of the day, and every one of Shakespeare's plays features portents and auspicious signs. Finally, a day was chosen to open the new playhouse. The sun and planets aligned and the theatre opened on the midsummer night's solstice: the 12th of June 1599. The premiere was a play also loaded with signs and portents: *Julius Caesar*. And a worthy name for this grand venture? The Globe.

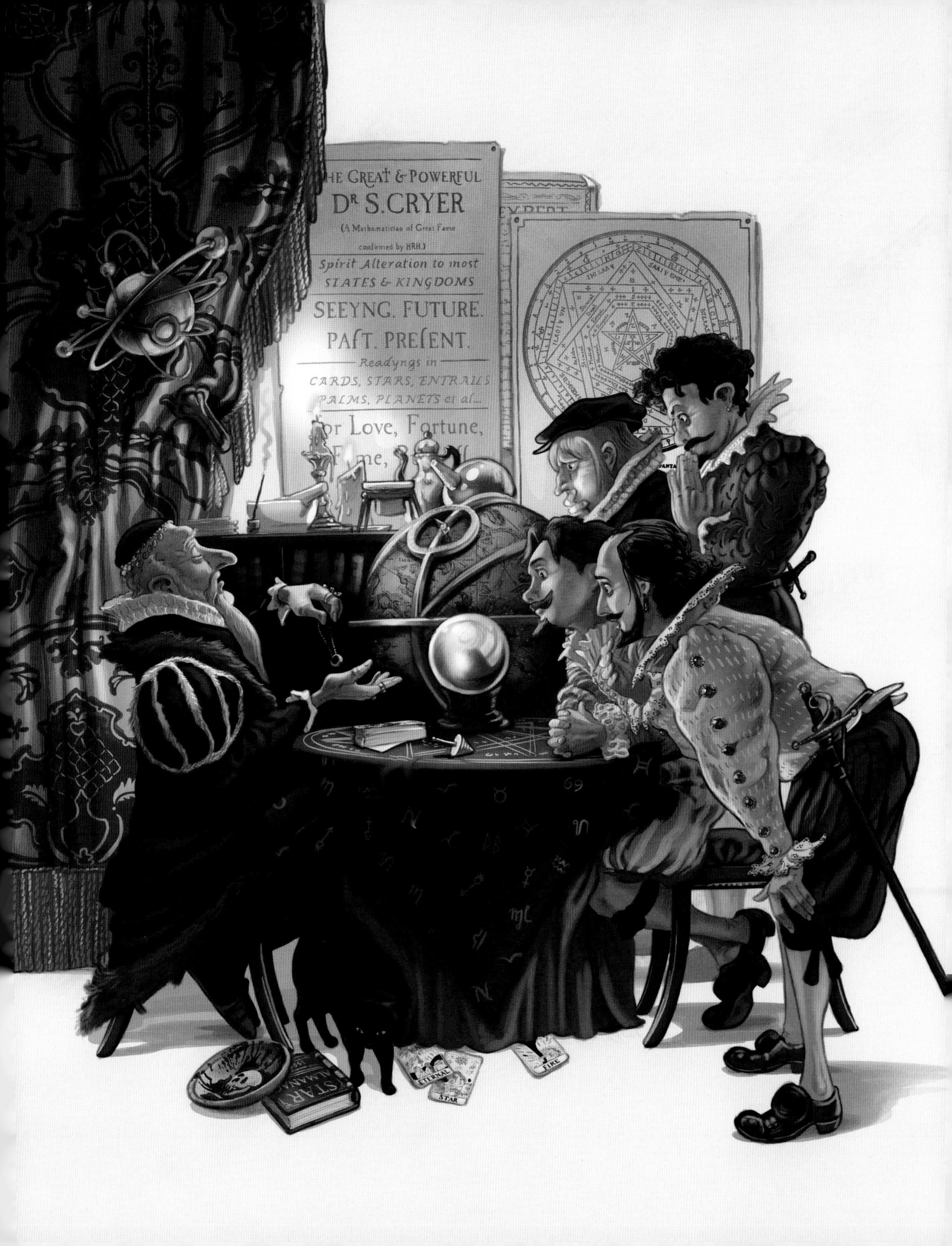

HE GREAT & POWERFUL
Dr S.CRYER
(A Mathematician of Great Fame
confirmed by HRH.)
Spirit Alteration to most
STATES & KINGDOMS
SEEYNG. FUTURE.
PAſT. PREſENT.
Readyngs in
CARDS, STARS, ENTRAILS
PALMS, PLANETS et al...
or Love, Fortune,
ETERNAL
STAR
FIRE

All that glisters is not gold.

THE MERCHANT OF VENICE

The Globe theatre quickly became *the* place to be. The theatre itself was decked out in grand theatrical fakery, with mock marble pillars and gilt embellishments — emulating the palace buildings which most of the audience wouldn't be allowed within a mile of. The costumes, on the other hand, were not mouldy outfits repurposed from previous performances. Instead the players wore real suits of armour and sumptuous garments, often donated hand-me-downs from the Court or noble households, some of which were worth a small fortune in themselves. The Globe was such a success that the nearby players (one hundred yards down the road at the Rose) packed up and moved to another theatre for a period, due to lost income.

Once more unto the breach, dear friends.

HENRY V

Will and the boys wowed the audiences, pulling out all their best plays. Now in his mid-thirties, Will proved his absolute mastery of history, comedy and tragedy with such diverse works as *Henry V*, *As You Like It* and *Hamlet*. With these crowd-pleasing shows and the opulent theatre, there was no competition from any other entertainment. The Globe could hold over 3000 people, who poured in from all walks of life: from the 'stinkards' and working classes to the merchants and courtiers, even a few of the nobility. Of course Will and his business partners were keen to capitalise with vendors pressing upon the throng ale, pipe tobacco and snacks.

Brevity is the soul of wit.

HAMLET

According to contemporary playwright Ben Jonson, Will was anything but brief. It was all part of their now mythical rivalry — Jonson was the classically trained poet, wed to structure and learning, whilst Shakespeare was the yokel with a natural untrained genius. Jonson claimed that Will lacked any learning, failing to recognise the immense skill he'd earned through sheer practice. Both were amongst a group of playwrights involved in a constant to and fro of parodies, satires, rip-offs and put-downs of each other's plays, which became known as the 'Poets' War'.

With the help of a surgeon he might yet recover, and prove an ass.

A MIDSUMMER NIGHT'S DREAM

The competing theatre troops were a bunch of hot-heads, all too ready to mouth off and slash before asking questions. At the turn of the century the brawl moved onstage as a battle of wits. In one case, playwright Ben Jonson poked fun at Shakespeare's newly acquired family coat of arms — a falcon with the motto 'not without right'. In Jonson's *Every Man out of His Humour*, one character purchases a coat of arms for £30 — it's a boar's head with the motto 'not without mustard'. It must have been a fairly friendly battle as Will is listed as an actor in two of Jonson's plays. But the rivalry continued after Will's death when Jonson had another dig at his fellow playwright, claiming that although the players would not have changed a single word, he (Jonson) wished Shakespeare had blotted a thousand lines.

Poison shows worst in a golden cup; dark night seems darker by the lightning flash; lilies that fester smell far worse than weeds.

KING EDWARD III

In 1601 Will and his colleagues came within a hair's breadth of losing their heads. The Earl of Essex paid them a wad of cash to perform one of Will's early plays, *Richard II*. This story, featuring banned scenes of abdication and regicide, was reported to be a signal for a public uprising to overthrow the government. However, the only ones who took up arms were the authorities, who were well aware of the incompetent plot.

Even a fleeting connection with this failed rebellion could have ended with the players' heads decorating London Bridge with all the other traitors — a gruesome show to all who passed the southern gate on their way to the Globe. Miraculously Will and the troupe were let off with only a slap on the wrist, as they claimed they were merely innocent players performing on request. Essex had been the Queen's golden boy at court, so his betrayal must have hit Elizabeth particularly hard, and he was rightly given the usual punishment for treason.

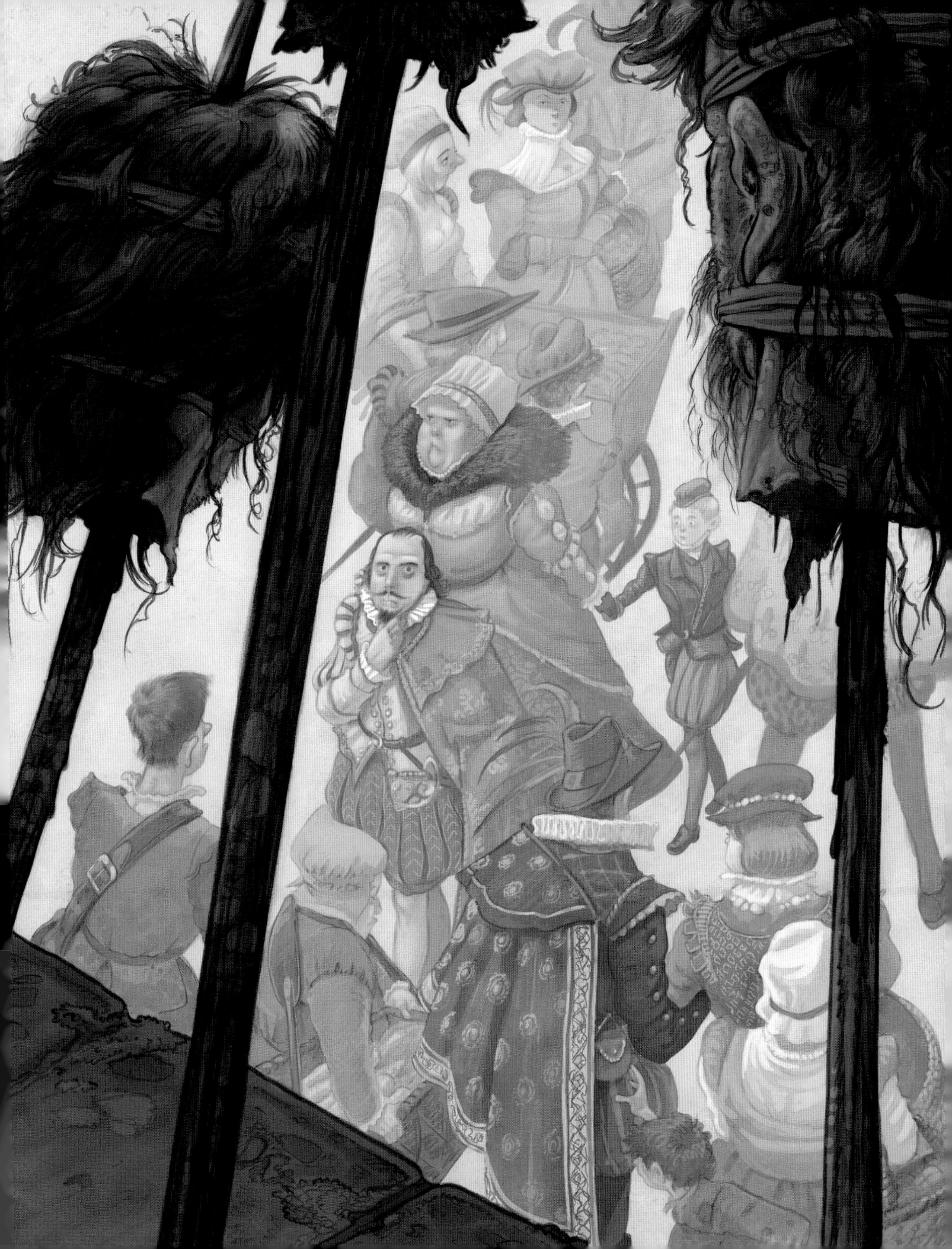

The world's mine oyster.
Which I with sword will open.

THE MERRY WIVES OF WINDSOR

When Queen Elizabeth died in 1603, Shakespeare was criticised for not composing anything to commemorate the Queen's passing. But where Liz had been merely fond of plays, new King James adored them. Will's troupe now became the 'King's Men' and were asked to perform frequently. As part of the royal entourage they were given four and a half yards of scarlet cloth to have new outfits tailored. But it wasn't all wine and oysters. On occasion the King's Men were required to swell the numbers at court, and were even asked to wait upon foreign dignitaries.

Will himself was now a national icon. Plays such as *Hamlet* were translated and performed across Europe — admired by everyone from the peasant groundlings to the university snobs. Will had elevated the theatre to the realm of literature.

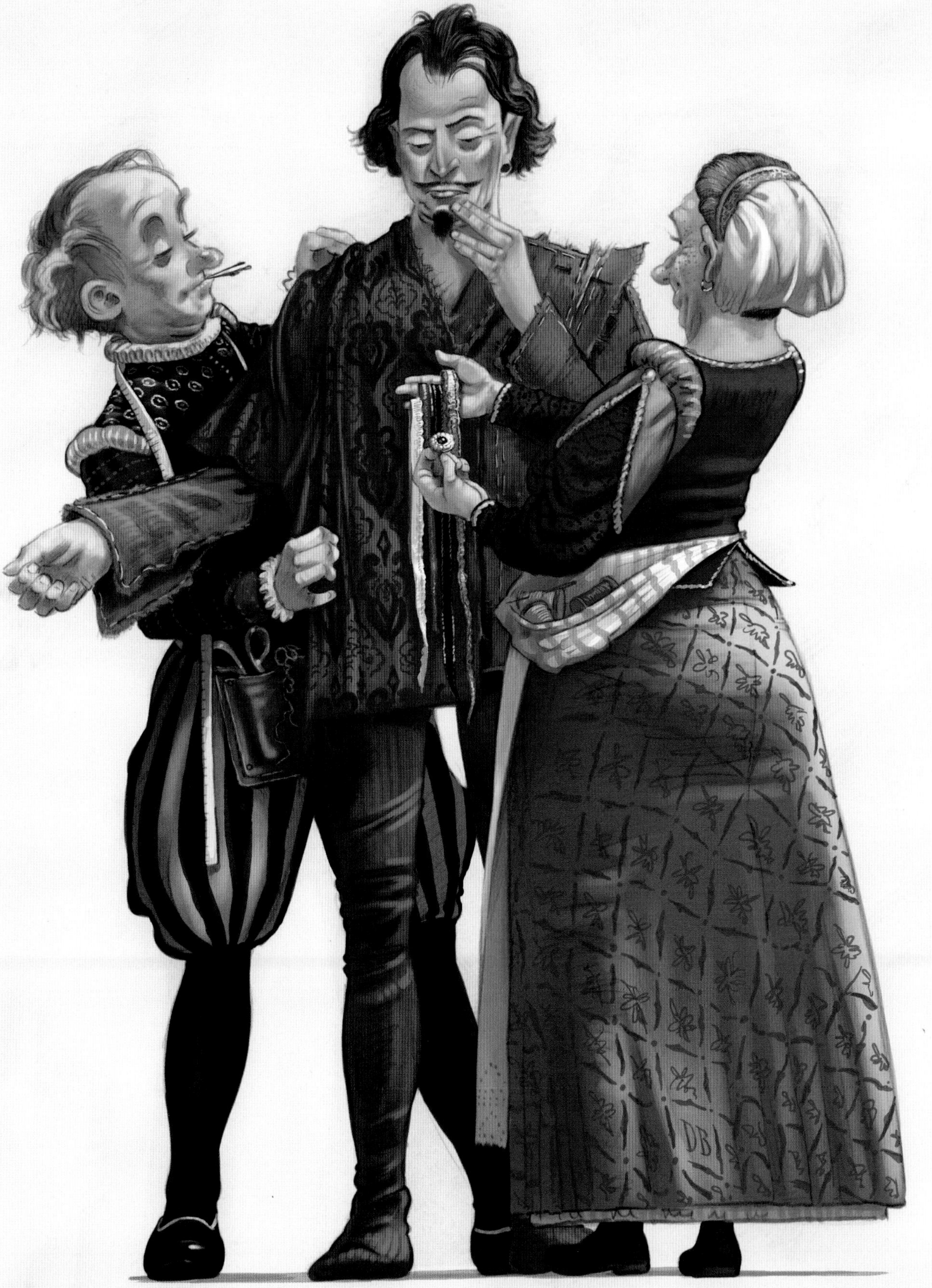

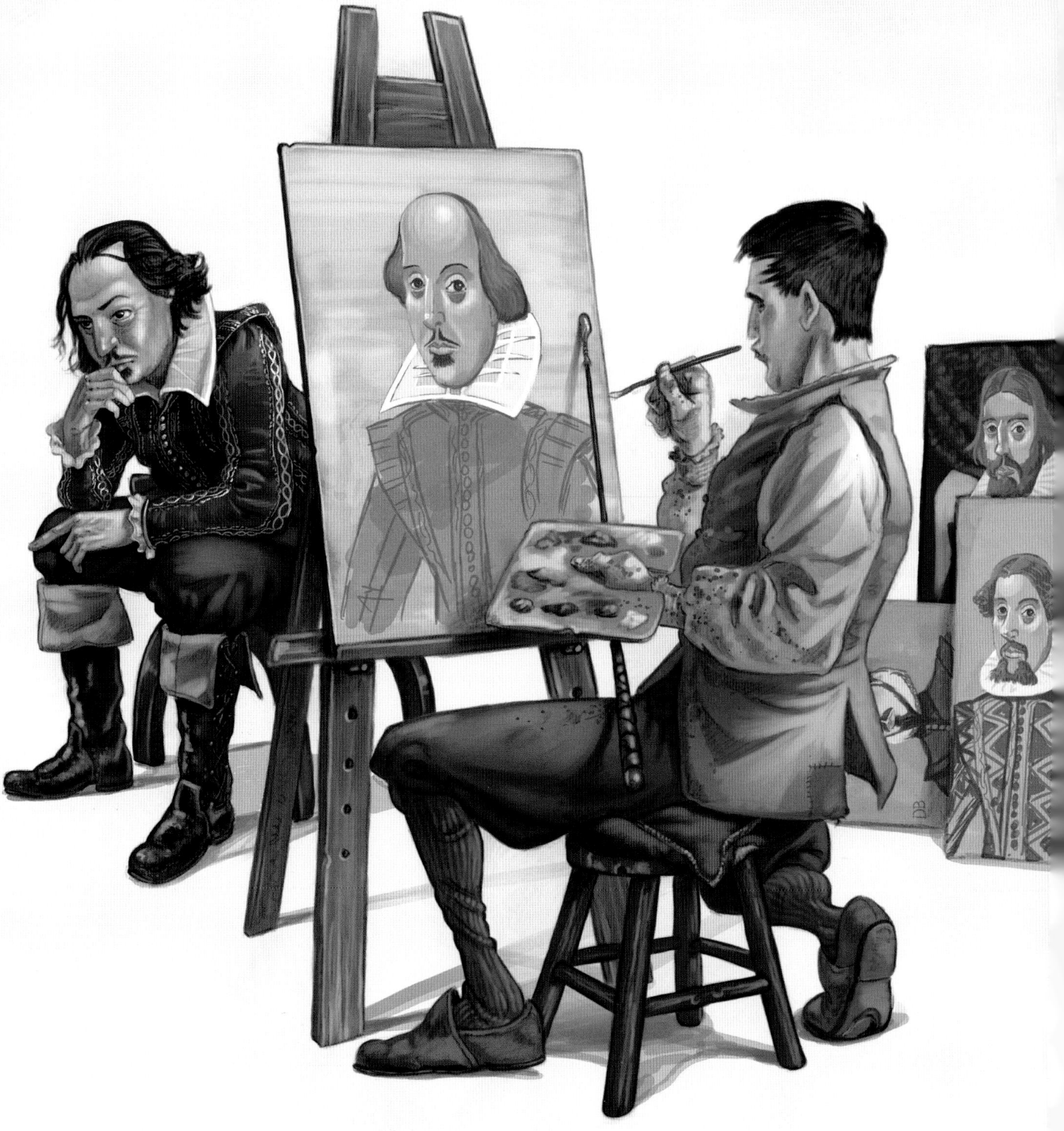

Yet eyes this cunning want to grace their art; they draw but what they see, know not the heart.

SONNET 24

There are no verified portraits of William Shakespeare that were made during his lifetime. The two likenesses we do have are the bust above his tomb in Stratford, and the famous Droeshout engraving which graces the title page of his first published works: the First Folio. The Droeshout portrait was claimed to be a fair likeness by Will's old friends who had put the publication together. But even this portrait was done in 1623, seven years after Will's death. How could it be a true likeness? The engraver, Martin Droeshout, was probably copying a painting made during Will's life, that has since been lost. In the style of the times, Will looks rather dour, and it's hard to picture the quick wit and fiery genius that is racing behind that stony poker face.

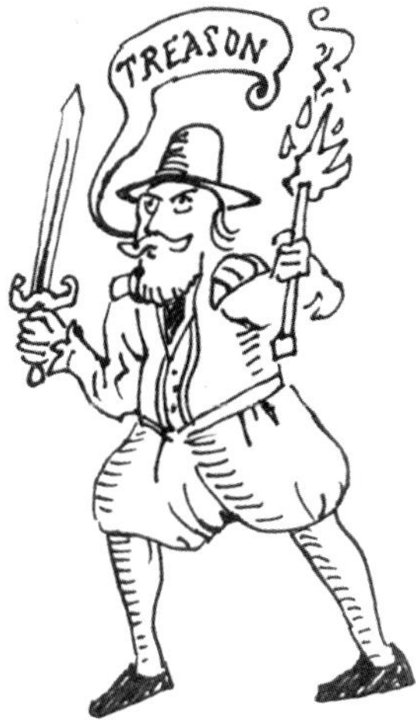
TREASON

'Zounds, I am afraid of this gunpowder.

HENRY IV PART ONE

Blood, guts, gore and veins in yer teeth. Early in 1606 the infamous Gunpowder Plotters were executed and in the most disgustingly brutal way. As hellish as we consider it now, this public spectacle was familiar to the London crowds and there was barely a man, woman or child who didn't turn out to witness it.

King James I was initially tolerant towards religious freedom, but now he came down hard on Catholics. This vicious round-up of conspirators would have been unsettling for Will's family back in Stratford, as some of the plotters were from his county of Warwickshire.

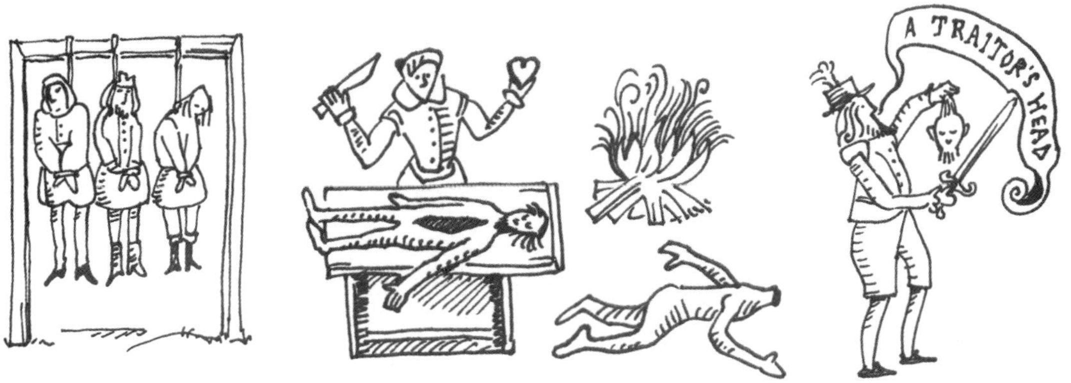
A TRAITOR'S HEAD

Some guard these traitors to the block of death, treason's true bed and yielder up of breath.

HENRY IV PART TWO

Macbeth was written in the aftermath of the Gunpowder Plot and Will proved to be a solid King's man — he knew what side his bread was buttered on. *Macbeth* tells us what happens to traitorous dogs who would be king. Will makes references to the show trials of the Gunpowder conspirators. He also plays up to the King's Scottish heritage as well as James' fascination with witches and the occult.

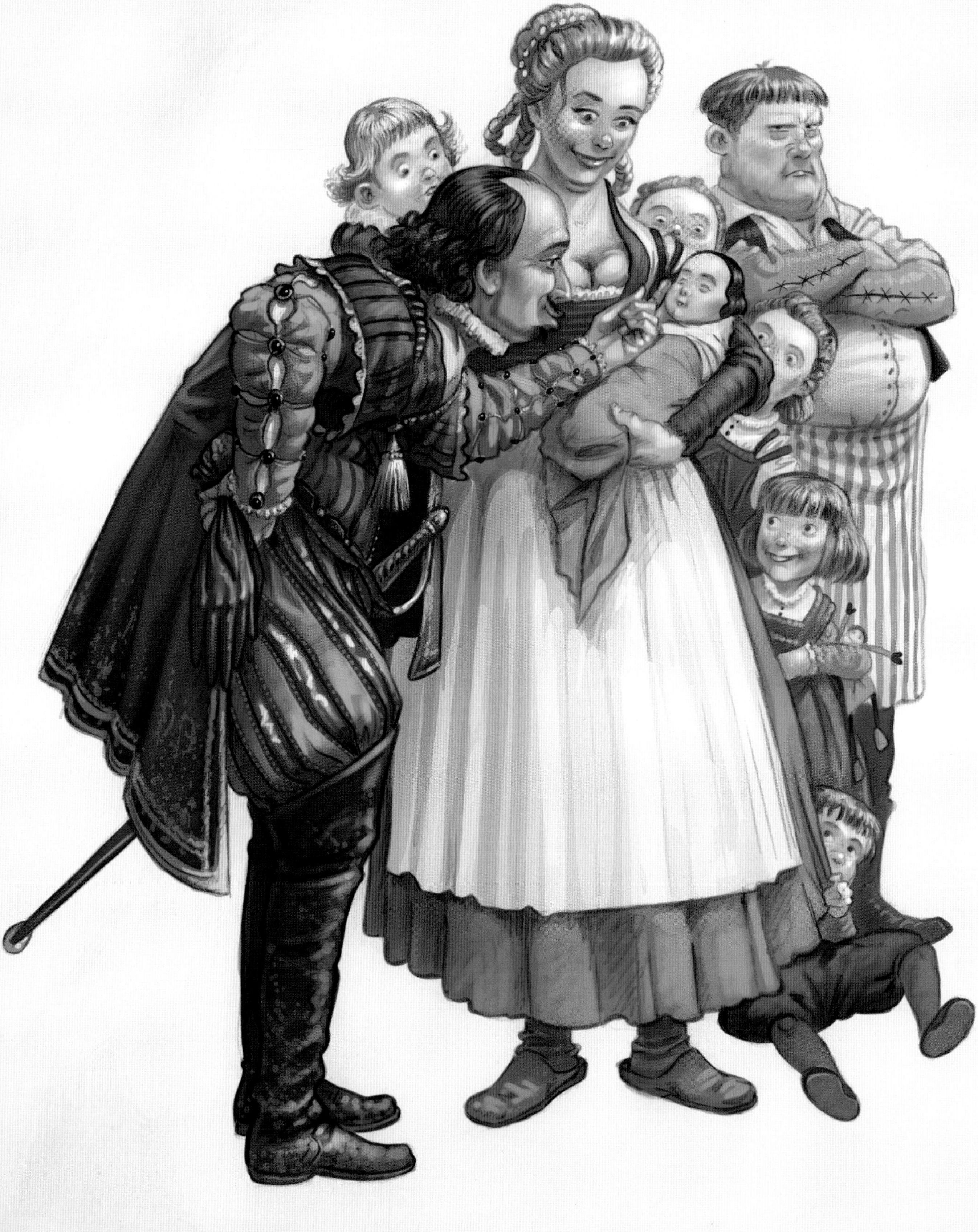

Our pleasant vices make instruments to scourge us.

KING LEAR

One of Will's pleasant vices was to stop off at an Oxford tavern when travelling between London and Stratford. Will became godfather to William Davenant, the tavern owner's second son, who had an uncanny, and possibly unsettling, resemblance to his namesake. Common gossip said that Will was the father, a fact that Will Junior was quick to play up when he later became a poet and playwright himself. Actually William Junior did much to keep Shakespeare's plays in public performance and appreciation during the seventeenth century.

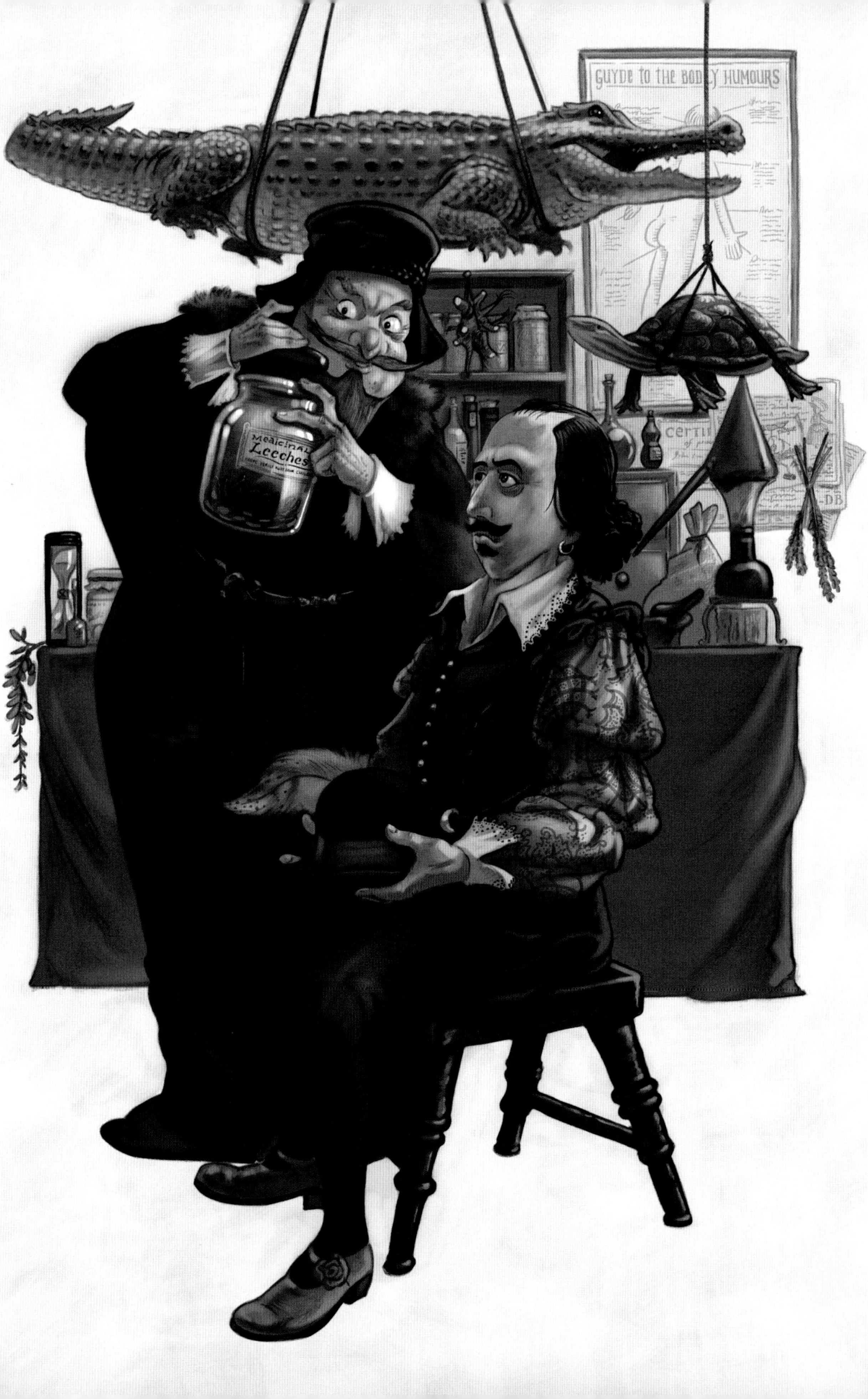
GUYDE TO THE
HUMOURS
Medicinal
Leeches
DB

Though this be madness, yet there is method in't.

HAMLET

Will was lucky to survive many outbreaks of the plague during his life, but there were plenty of other threats to worry about too. Diseases such as typhus, malaria, smallpox and syphilis were bad enough — and the cures could be worse than the cause. Remedies such as mercury treatment, arsenic, powdered hedgehog testicles, the ever-popular leeches, along with dung of all kinds, seem more madness than method to our modern senses. Mind you, this was top-notch medicine from a real doctor, not just any old quack. In 1607 Will's eldest daughter, Susanna, made a respectable marriage to Stratford doctor John Hall. From this period on, Will's plays show a detailed knowledge of all the current medical trends.

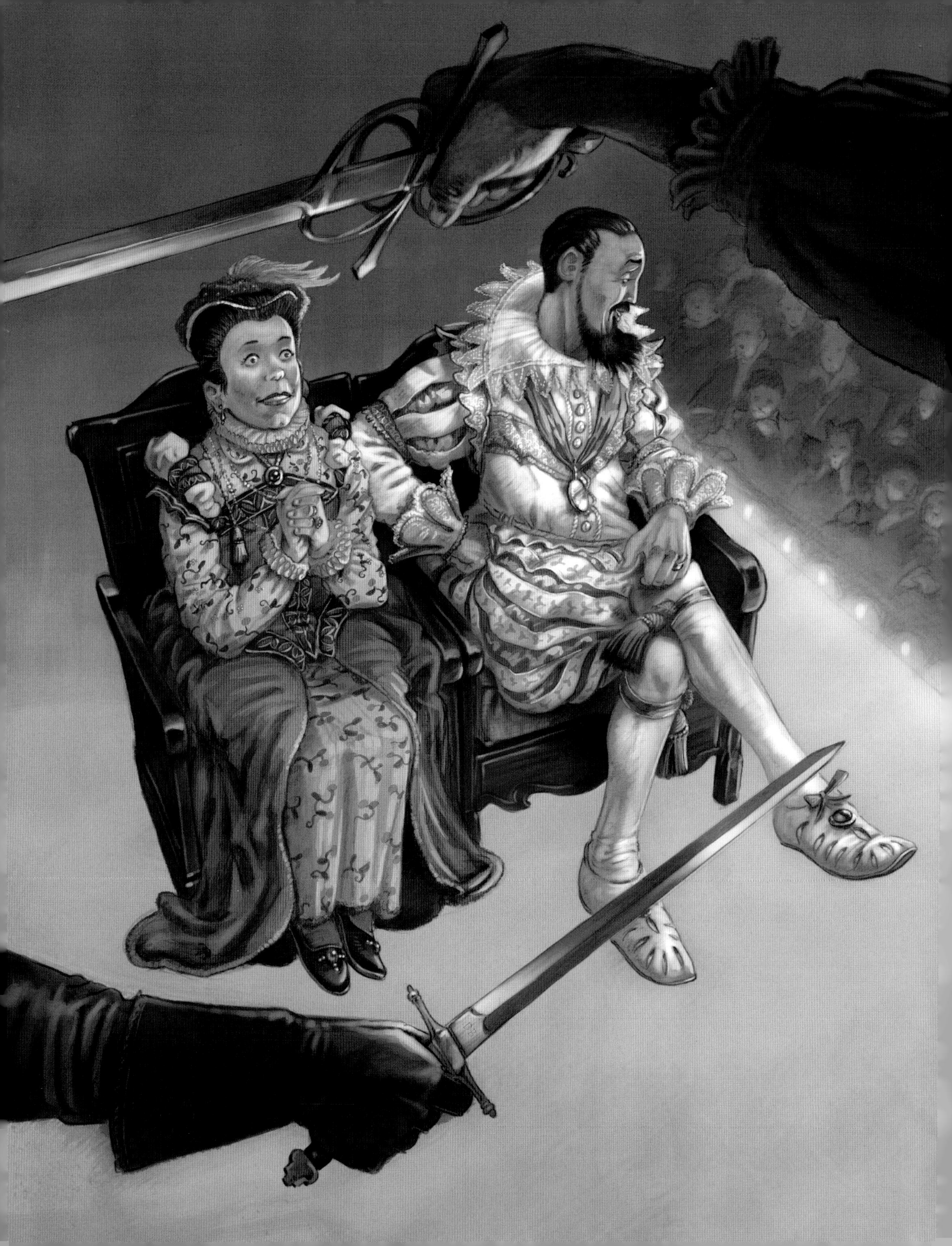

All the world's a stage, and all the men and women merely players.

AS YOU LIKE IT

In 1609 Richard Burbage, Will and their fellow sharers began performances at their Blackfriars Theatre, a purpose-built indoor playhouse, just down the road from St Paul's Cathedral. This swanky new venue became the template for all modern theatres, with artificial lighting and new theatrical effects. It was a much more intimate theatre than the Globe and, for an extra fee, men and women from the audience could even be seated on stage with the players. Here they could see better — as well as be seen better.

The new theatre was a lucrative earner for Will, who took one sixth of the profits. Now they could perform all through the winter to the wealthy, as well as run summer months at the Globe. Between the two venues Will and the King's Men ruled the London crowds.

Take heed,
lest by your heat
you burn yourselves.

HENRY VI PART TWO

In 1613 the Globe was still the hottest place to be. With elaborate costumes and dinky new props they had silenced the competition. But on the 29th of June one of these props — a stage cannon — accidentally fired, setting the thatch roof alight. It was during a performance of one of Will's last plays, the collaborative effort that was *Henry VIII*. The Globe was consumed in less than two hours. One playgoer noted that no one was injured, but one man, whose breeches caught fire had the provident wit to put out the flames with a bottle of ale.

Will, as a one-fourteenth partner, was up for £60 as his share of the rebuilding costs. Within a year the Globe was up and running again, but this time without Will. He'd decided that this incident was an opportunity to sell his shares in both the troupe and the Globe, effectively retiring from the theatre.

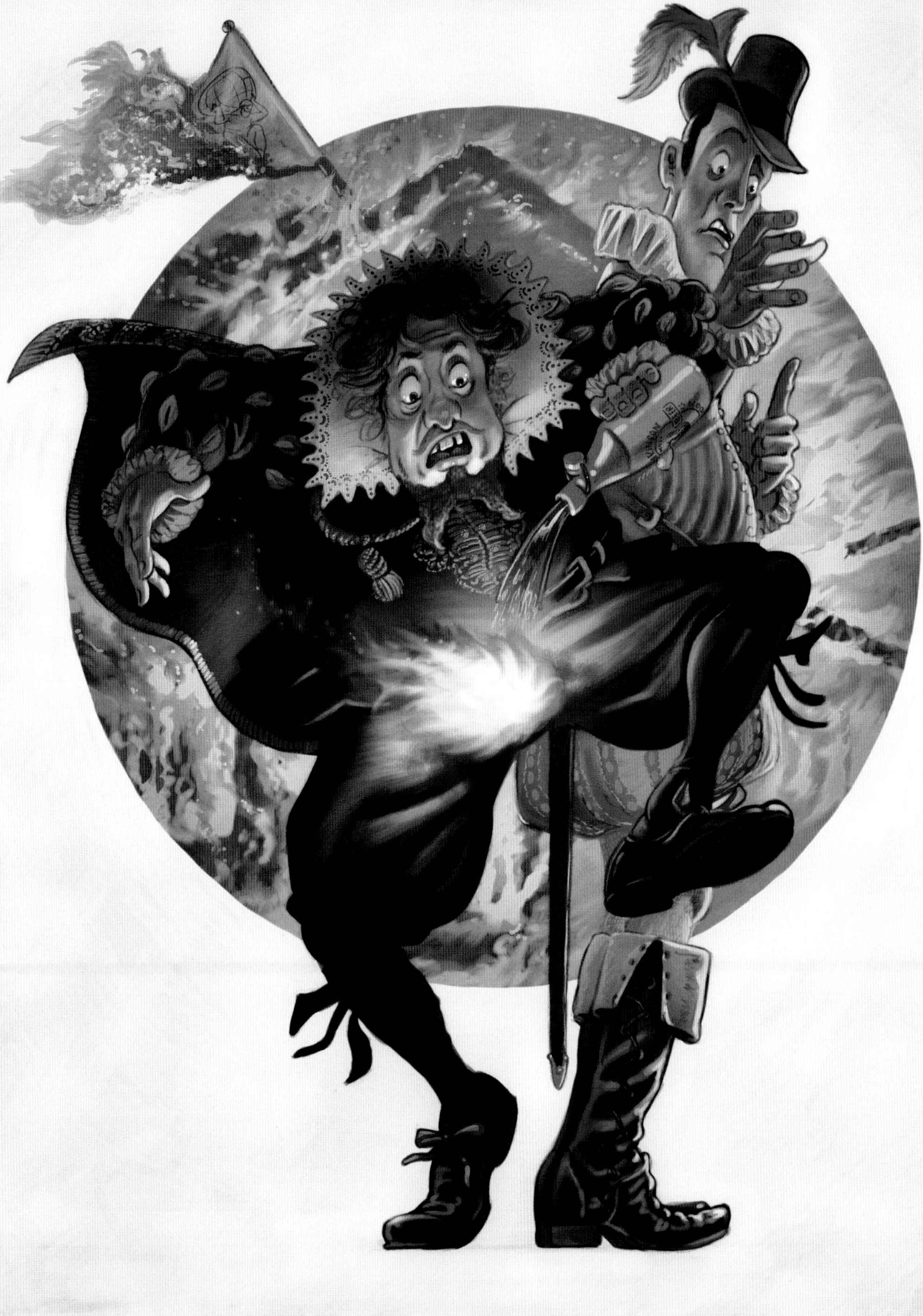

Life's but a walking shadow, a poor player that struts and frets his hour upon the stage and then is heard no more.

MACBETH

Some historians claim that Will all but abandoned his family for the London theatre scene. If so, why did he return to Stratford? He still had a London house in Blackfriars, which he had bought in 1613, but after the Globe fire, Will appears to have given up writing plays altogether and his voice was heard no more. The Stratford countryside pulled him home. Was it to oversee his various investment properties and hoard grain stores to push up the value? He was certainly accused of the latter. But he also had his grand country house, New Place, with its gardens and orchards, and, of course, his family.

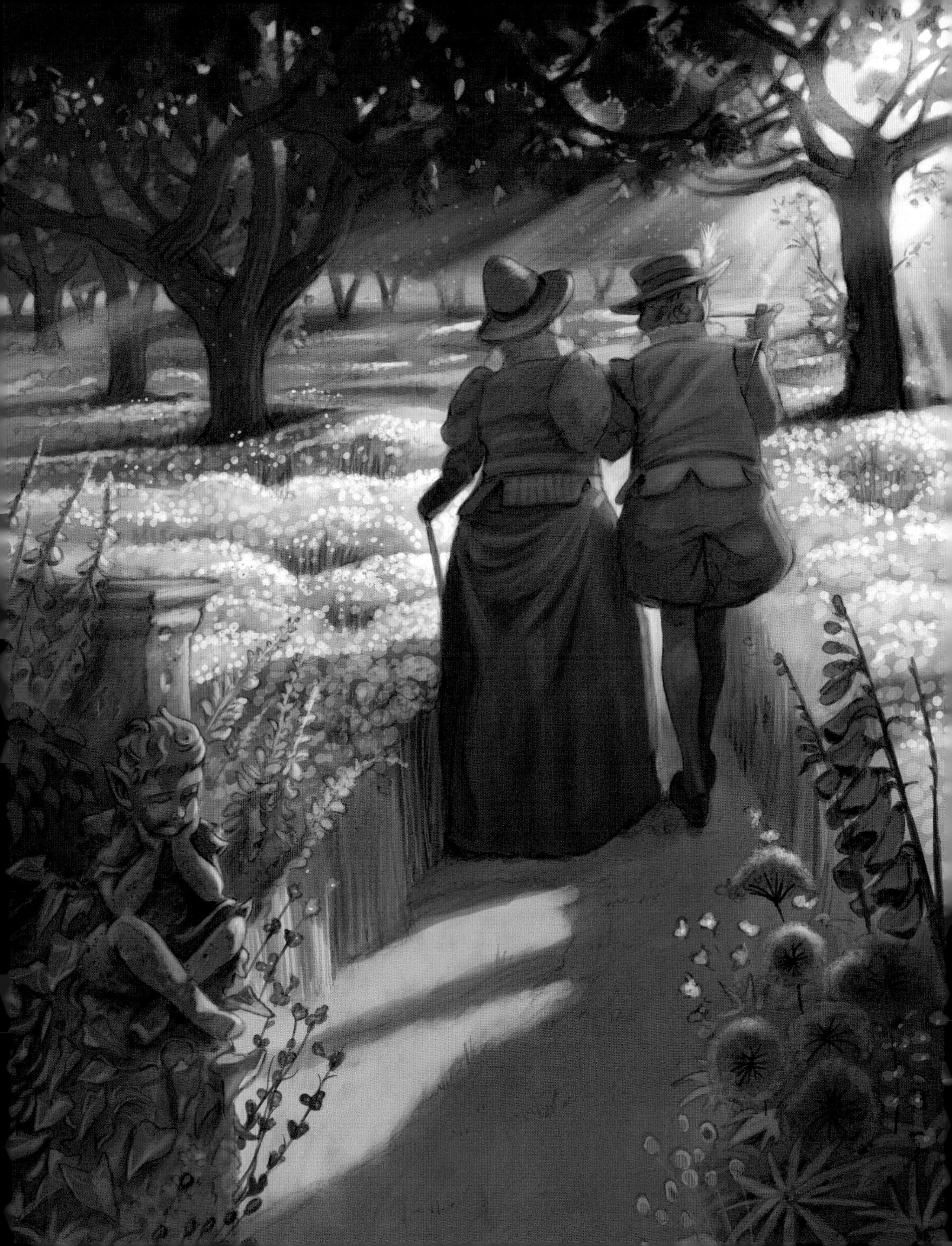

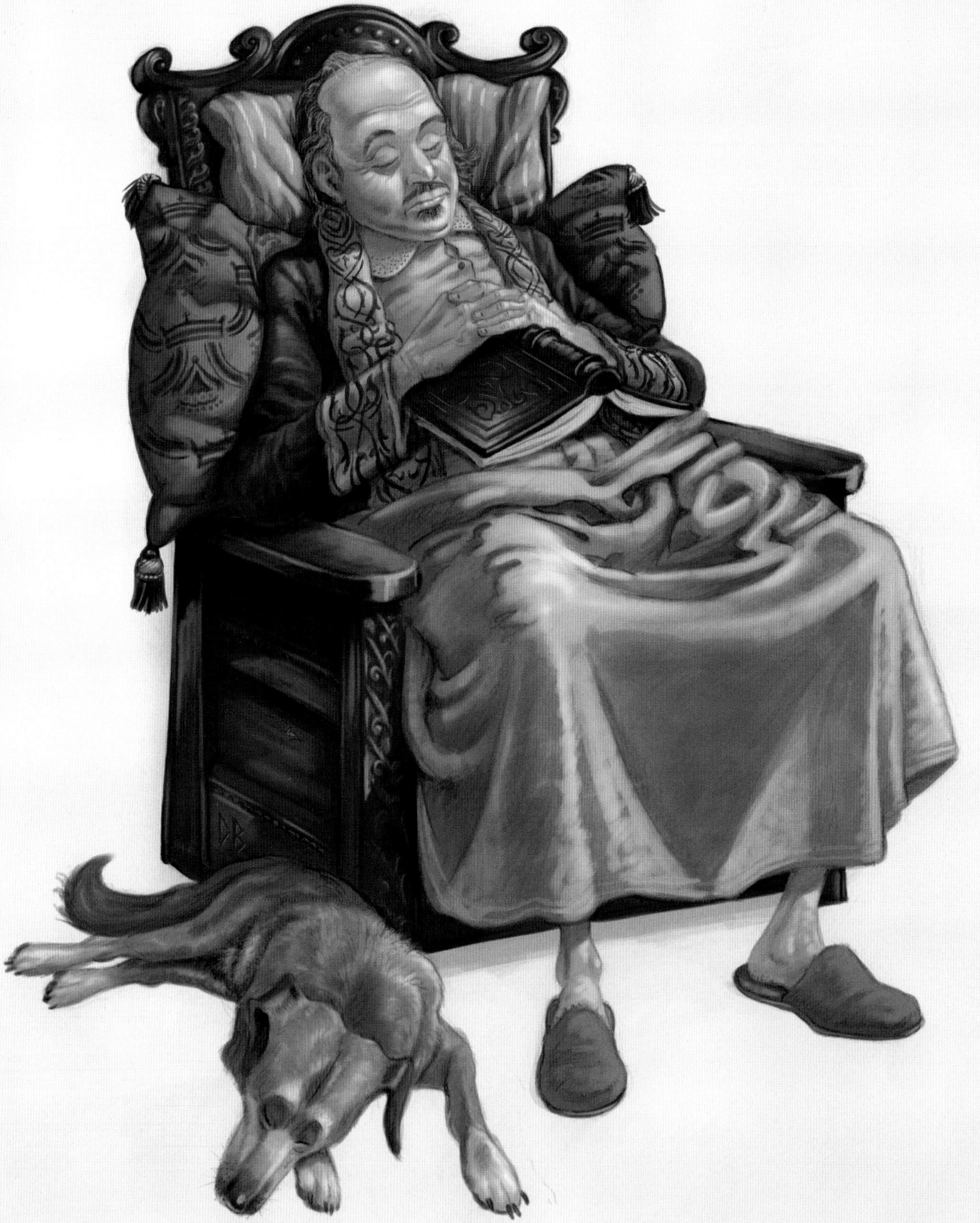

The wheel has come full circle.

KING LEAR

By 1614 Will had long missed his own children's childhoods. At fifty he was a granddad, an old man who had well surpassed the average life expectancy. His sonnets had been published in 1609 and it's possible that he spent his last years revising his plays for publication. After his death, his friends John Heminges and Henry Condell compiled a definitive complete works, known as the 'First Folio'. This lasting testament appeared at the Frankfurt Book Fair of 1623, seven years after Will's death.

Done to death
by slanderous tongues.

MUCH ADO ABOUT NOTHING

Shakespeare's final months were full of scandal. It must have been a shock to the system when Will learnt that his son-in-law, Thomas Quiney (who had recently married Will's younger daughter Judith), had had an affair with a village girl. To make matters worse, the poor girl died in childbirth, along with the baby. On the 25th of March 1616 Will rewrote his will, cutting Quiney out of any inheritance. Quiney was temporarily excommunicated from the church and ordered to serve public penance in front of the congregation. He got off with a fine, but it must have caused embarrassment and stress to Will, who had spent a lifetime establishing himself as a gent about town.

Within a month, Will was dead. The cause is unknown, but for hundreds of years the slanders kept coming. It was claimed that he died from syphilis or from a serious bout of hard drinking with his old theatre mates, amongst other things. The fact is, there are no facts. Susanna's daughter Elizabeth was the only grandchild alive at the time, and was also Will's last surviving descendant. It's a shame that no one sought her out for recollections of her grandfather.

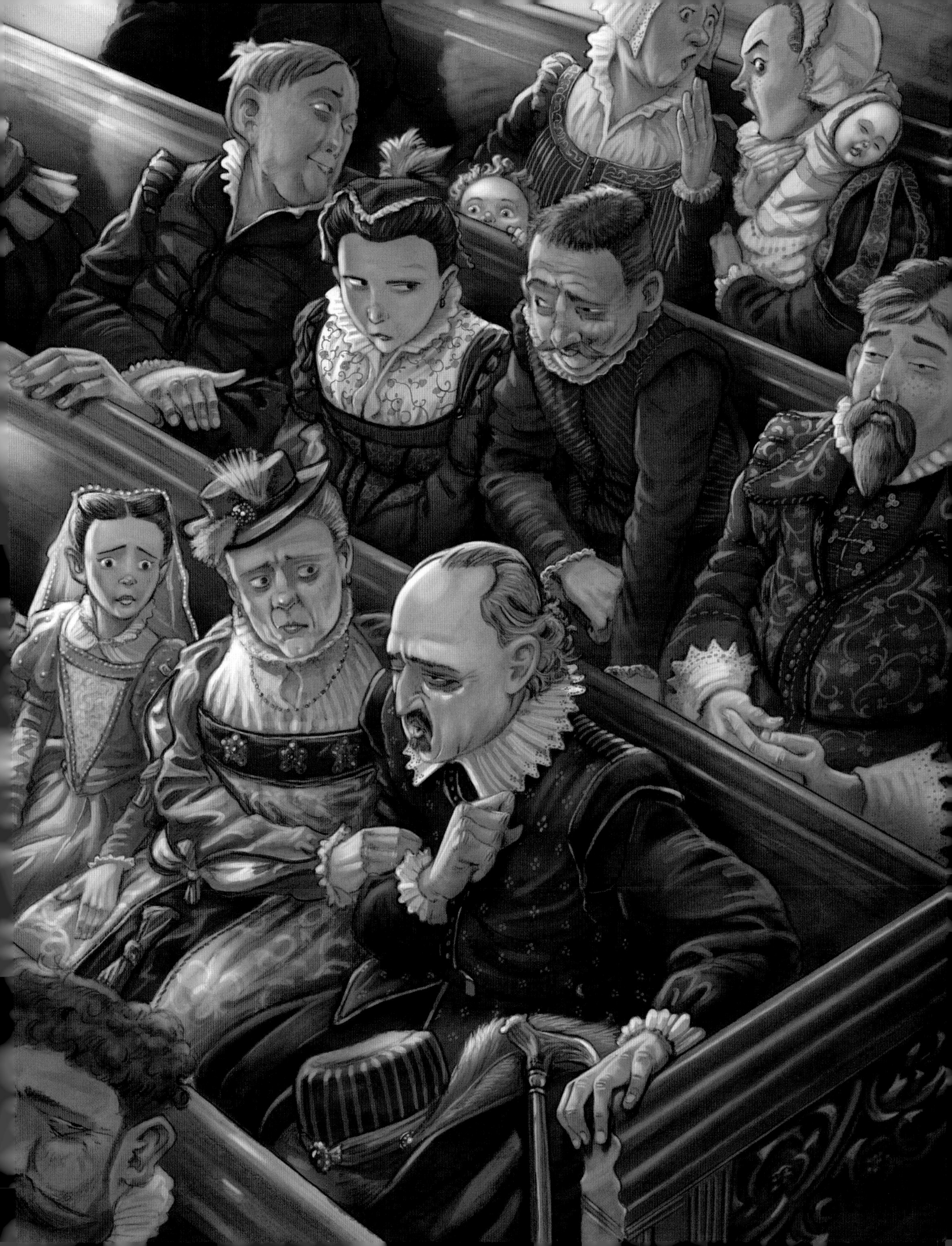

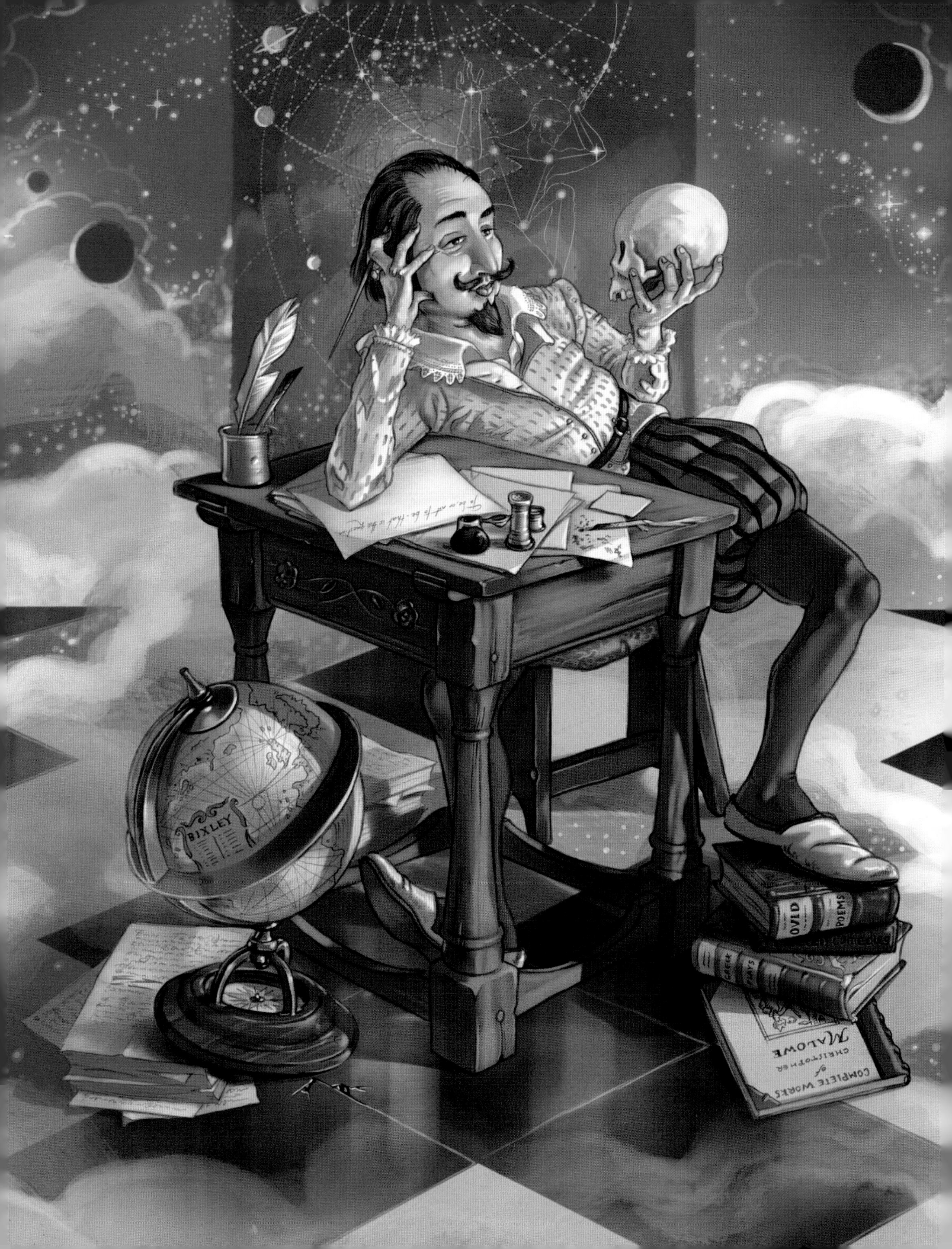
BIXLEY
OVID
POEMS
GREEK PLAYS
COMPLETE WORKS of CHRISTOPHER MARLOWE

To die, to sleep.
To sleep perchance to dream:
ay, there's the rub!
For in that sleep of death
what dreams may come
when we have shuffled off
this mortal coil.

HAMLET

Will was incredibly successful during his lifetime, but he could never have dreamed what legendary status he would gain after his death. In 1616 Will added to his own legend by shuffling off this mortal coil on the most auspicious of days, the 23rd of April. Not only was it mythically the same date he came into the world, but also St George's Day. What could be more fitting for England's future 'Man of the Millennium' than to be born and die on England's national day? Will had just turned fifty-two, over the average expected lifespan, but certainly not old by today's standards. Unusually, he was buried seventeen feet down, which some scholars claim suggests he died of a contagious disease. His tomb is in the Holy Trinity Church in Stratford-upon-Avon, often called 'Shakespeare's Church'.

GOOD FRIEND FOR

TO DIGG THE

BLEST BE THE MAN

AND CVRST BE

JESVS SAKE FORBEAR,
DVST ENCLOSED HERE.
THAT SPARES THESE STONES
HE THAT MOVES MY BONES.

Shakespeare's epitaph

Timeline

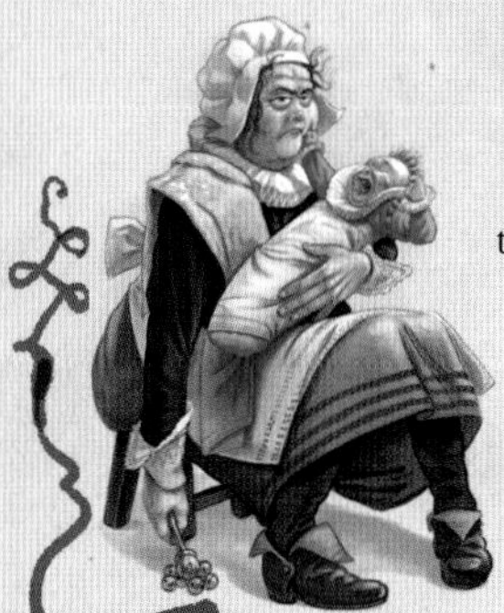

1564
William Shakespeare, the first surviving child of John and Mary, is born and is baptised on 26th of April.

1568 AGE 4
Shakespeare's father becomes mayor of Stratford.

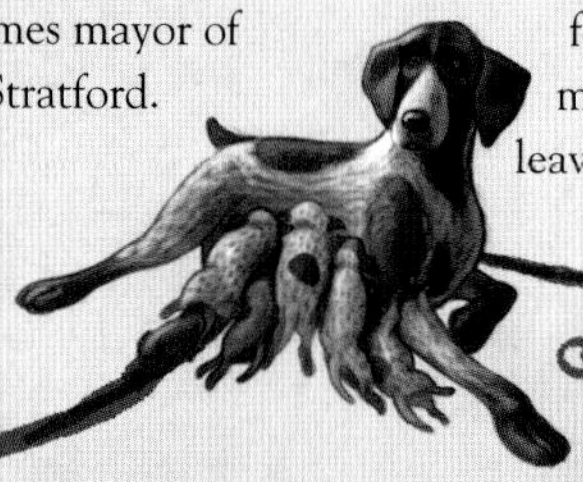

1576 AGE 12
The Theatre, England's first sole-purpose playhouse, is built in Shoreditch, just north of London's city walls. Shakespeare will go on to perform there. John, Will's father, is prosecuted for illegal wool trading and illegally lending money. This, combined with some bad debts, leaves the Shakespeares almost completely broke.

1593 AGE 29
William Shakespeare appears for the first time as a named author with the publication of *Venus and Adonis*, which will go on to be his most successful publication in his lifetime. Christopher Marlowe is stabbed to death in a tavern brawl. Plague closes the theatres.

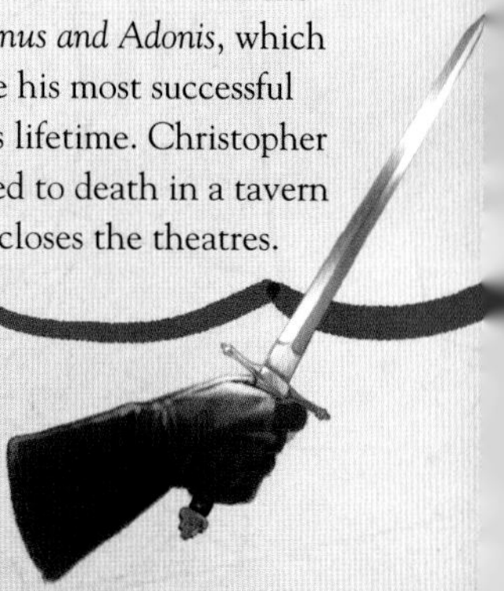

1594 AGE 30
The playhouses are reopened and Shakespeare becomes part of the Lord Chamberlain's Men, who regularly perform at court.

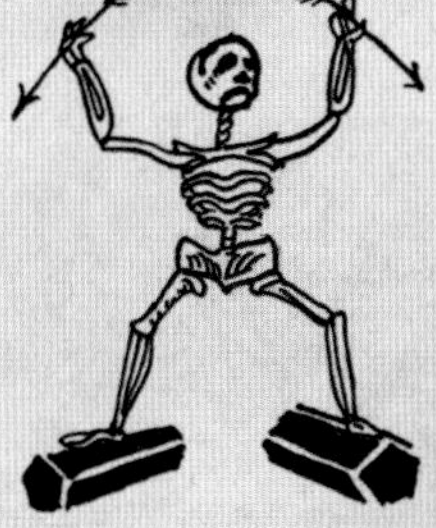

1596 AGE 32
In August, Will and Anne's eleven-year-old son, Hamnet, dies. The Shakespeare family are granted a coat of arms.

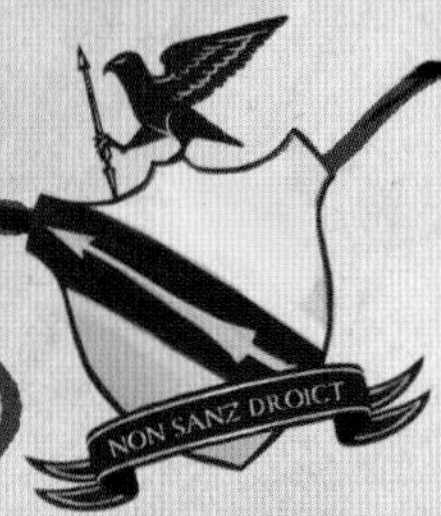
NON SANZ DROICT

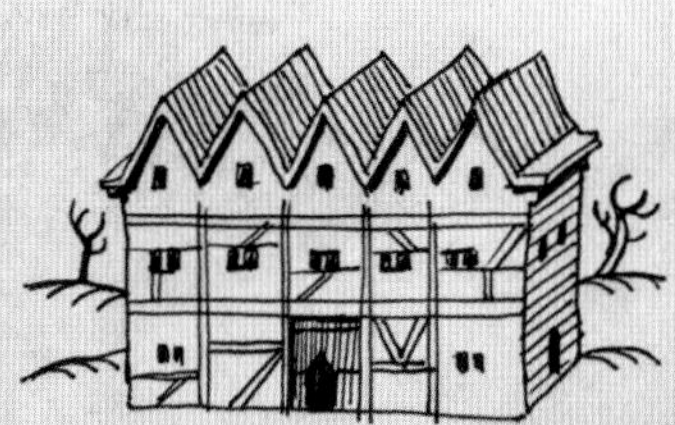

1597 AGE 33
Will purchases New Place as the family home, one of the grandest houses in Stratford.

1598 AGE 34
Love's Labour's Lost is the first surviving record of a play to be published in Shakespeare's name. Shakespeare's company loses the lease on the land where the Theatre stands. They dismantle the playhouse and relocate to Southwark, on the south side of the Thames.

1599 AGE 35
In June, the rebuilt playhouse opens as the Globe. Will is now a partner sharing profits in both the playhouse and the troupe.

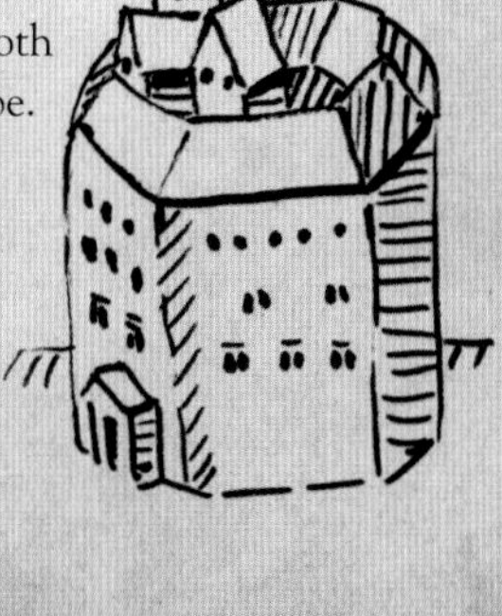

1601 AGE 37
Shakespeare's company perform the treasonable play *Richard II*, and are implicated in the Earl of Essex's revolt. Essex is beheaded. Will's father dies.

1603 AGE 39
Elizabeth I dies and is succeeded by James I. Will's company become known as the King's Men, performing often at court.

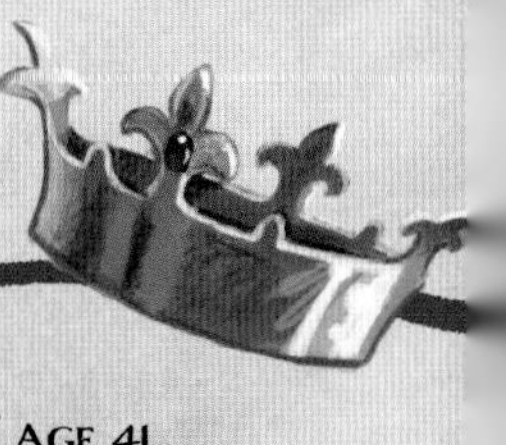

1605 AGE 41
Guy Fawkes and his co-conspirators try to blow up the Houses of Parliament with their Gunpowder Plot.

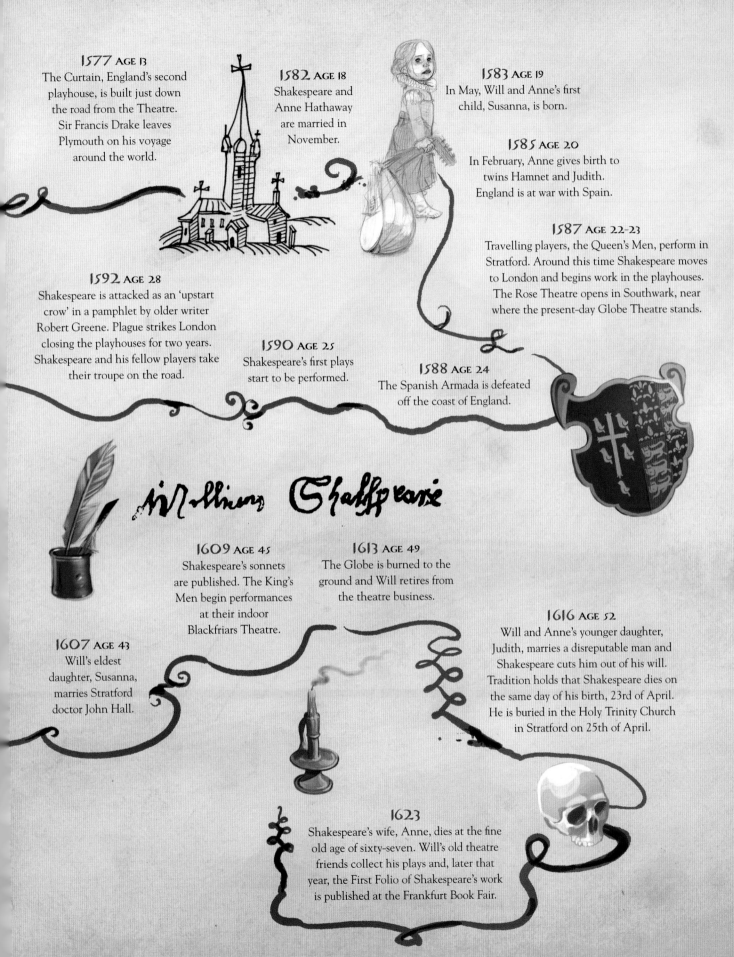

1577 AGE 13
The Curtain, England's second playhouse, is built just down the road from the Theatre. Sir Francis Drake leaves Plymouth on his voyage around the world.

1582 AGE 18
Shakespeare and Anne Hathaway are married in November.

1583 AGE 19
In May, Will and Anne's first child, Susanna, is born.

1585 AGE 20
In February, Anne gives birth to twins Hamnet and Judith. England is at war with Spain.

1587 AGE 22–23
Travelling players, the Queen's Men, perform in Stratford. Around this time Shakespeare moves to London and begins work in the playhouses. The Rose Theatre opens in Southwark, near where the present-day Globe Theatre stands.

1592 AGE 28
Shakespeare is attacked as an 'upstart crow' in a pamphlet by older writer Robert Greene. Plague strikes London closing the playhouses for two years. Shakespeare and his fellow players take their troupe on the road.

1590 AGE 25
Shakespeare's first plays start to be performed.

1588 AGE 24
The Spanish Armada is defeated off the coast of England.

1609 AGE 45
Shakespeare's sonnets are published. The King's Men begin performances at their indoor Blackfriars Theatre.

1613 AGE 49
The Globe is burned to the ground and Will retires from the theatre business.

1616 AGE 52
Will and Anne's younger daughter, Judith, marries a disreputable man and Shakespeare cuts him out of his will. Tradition holds that Shakespeare dies on the same day of his birth, 23rd of April. He is buried in the Holy Trinity Church in Stratford on 25th of April.

1607 AGE 43
Will's eldest daughter, Susanna, marries Stratford doctor John Hall.

1623
Shakespeare's wife, Anne, dies at the fine old age of sixty-seven. Will's old theatre friends collect his plays and, later that year, the First Folio of Shakespeare's work is published at the Frankfurt Book Fair.

Shakespeare's Work

It is impossible to know the exact order of Shakespeare's plays because there is no record of any first production dates. However, scholars have estimated a chronology based on such things as historical events mentioned in the plays, records of performances by theatre managers and playgoers, and the dates that the plays first appeared in print. Listed below is one possible order.

1590-2	Henry VI, Part I	1599	Julius Caesar
	Henry VI, Part II	1600	As You Like It
	Henry VI, Part III		Twelfth Night
1592-3	Richard III	1600-1	Hamlet
	Titus Andronicus		Troilus and Cressida
	Venus and Adonis (poem)	1602-3	All's Well That Ends Well
1593-4	The Comedy of Errors		Othello
	The Taming of the Shrew	1604	Measure for Measure
	The Rape of Lucrece (poem)	1605-6	Timon of Athens
1594-5	Two Gentlemen of Verona		Macbeth
	Love's Labour's Lost		King Lear
1595-6	Romeo and Juliet	1607	Antony and Cleopatra
	Richard II	1608	Coriolanus
	A Midsummer Night's Dream	1609	Pericles
1596-7	King John	1610	Cymbeline
	The Merchant of Venice	1611	The Winter's Tale
1597-8	Henry IV, Part I	1612	The Tempest
	Henry IV, Part II	1613	Henry VIII*
1598-9	Much Ado About Nothing	1613	The Two Noble Kinsmen*
	Henry V		
	The Merry Wives of Windsor		*Co-written with John Fletcher

The quotes in this book have been used out of context. For a complete list of how they appear in Shakespeare's plays, visit www.donovanbixley.com/shakespeare

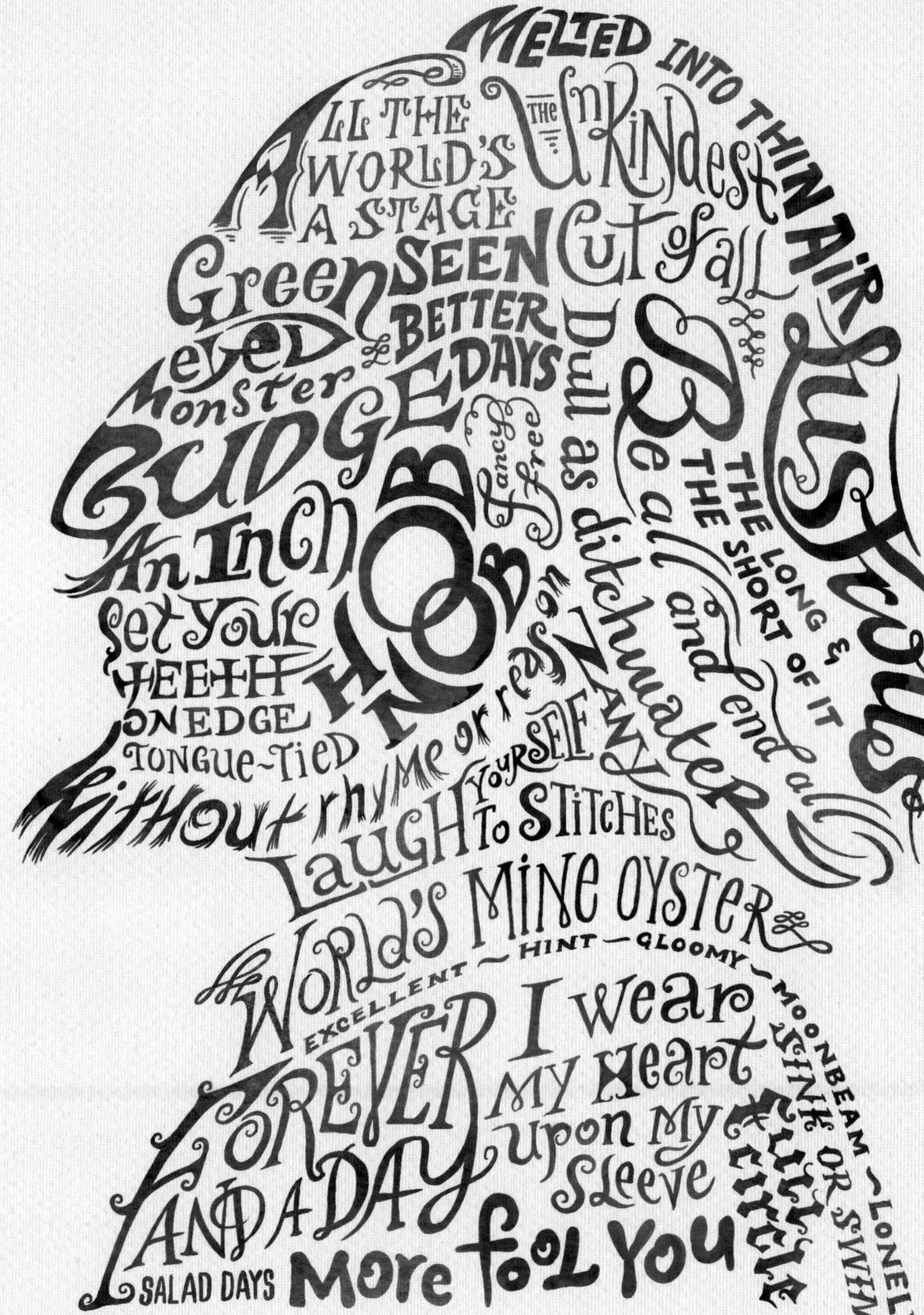
Melted into thin air
All the world's a stage
The unkindest cut of all
Green eyed monster
Seen better days
Budge an inch
Fancy free
Dull as ditchwater
Be all and end all
The long & the short of it
Lustrous
Set your teeth on edge
Hob nob
Tongue-tied
Without rhyme or reason
Zany
Laugh yourself to stitches
The world's mine oyster
Excellent ~ Hint ~ Gloomy ~ Moonbeam ~ Lonely
Forever and a day
I wear my heart upon my sleeve
Sink or swim
Full circle
Salad days
More fool you

If we shadows have offended,
Think but this, and all is mended,
That you have but slumbered here
While these visions did appear.

A MIDSUMMER NIGHT'S DREAM

Afterword

The absolute concrete facts about William Shakespeare are, to put it bluntly, not much. Over the last 400 years, though, an amazing amount of academic detective work and much obsessive document searching by some incredible fanatics have thrown up traces and hints and the ghost of William Shakespeare here and there. With this book, I've tried to capture those ghosts of Shakespeare's life and times, and pictures were the gateway into that world.

I wanted to depict a side of Shakespeare, the man, that we are not usually presented. Not the sainted genius, but big brother, drunk and disorderly teen, young lover, husband, father, bar-room brawler, tax evader, even grumpy old man. In short, although we don't know much about William Shakespeare, we do know that he was a real man. Like any of us, he was not a one-dimensional character, but made up of many parts which he played and showed to different people at different times.

Stylistically, I wanted to present Shakespeare's life and times in the same kind of theatrical fakery that his plays were presented at the Globe — for the most part, just bare stages with the characters wearing only their costumes and expressions. In the case of this book the pictures are also a puzzle for the quick-witted, with many in-jokes to decipher.

In the tradition of Shakespearean reinvention, I wanted to show Shakespeare and his world in a new light. What would a great humanist painter such as Norman Rockwell have made of Elizabethan England? And imagine how different our view of that period would be if it had been painted by Monet or Degas. I've certainly had fun overlaying Shakespeare's world with anachronisms and modern sensibilities.

I hope I have not offended. I hope you had fun. I hope you learned something. I hope that I brought to life a William Shakespeare who was not alone in the world, but a great man with that real human connection which is so apparent in his plays.

About the author

Donovan Bixley is one of New Zealand's most acclaimed picture-book creators with numerous awards and accolades to his name, being both an award-winning illustrator and an award-winning author. His work is nothing if not varied, spanning high-brow to low-brow and every brow in between, from his sublime illustrated biography *Faithfully Mozart*, to the ridiculous hi-jinks of feline aviators in *Flying Furballs*.

When not immersed in the world of picture books, Donovan plays saxophone, piano and guitar. He has performed on stage as Marius in *Les Misérables* and also worked behind the scenes as a set designer and painter. He lives in Taupo, New Zealand, with his wife and three daughters.

A catalogue record for this book is available
from the National Library of New Zealand

ISBN 978-1-927262-02-3

An Upstart Press Book
Published in 2016 by Upstart Press Ltd
B3, 72 Apollo Drive, Rosedale
Auckland, New Zealand

Printed by Everbest Printing Co. Ltd., China